JAPAN

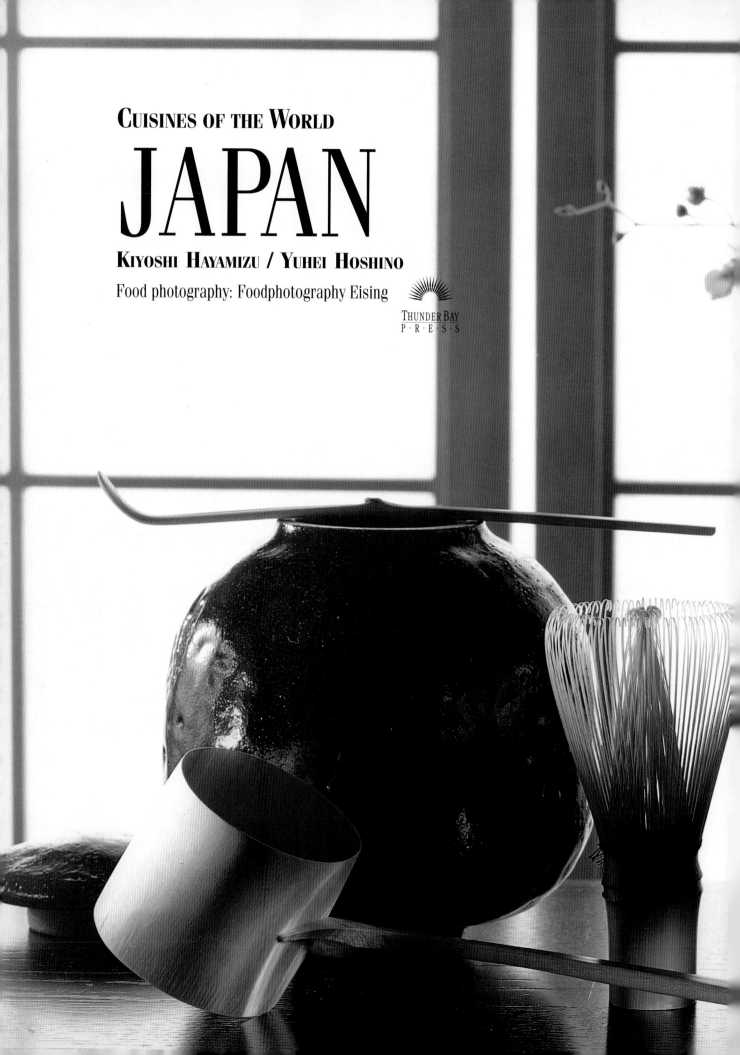

CUISINES OF THE WORLD

JAPAN

KIYOSHI HAYAMIZU / YUHEI HOSHINO

Food photography: Foodphotography Eising

THUNDER BAY
P·R·E·S·S

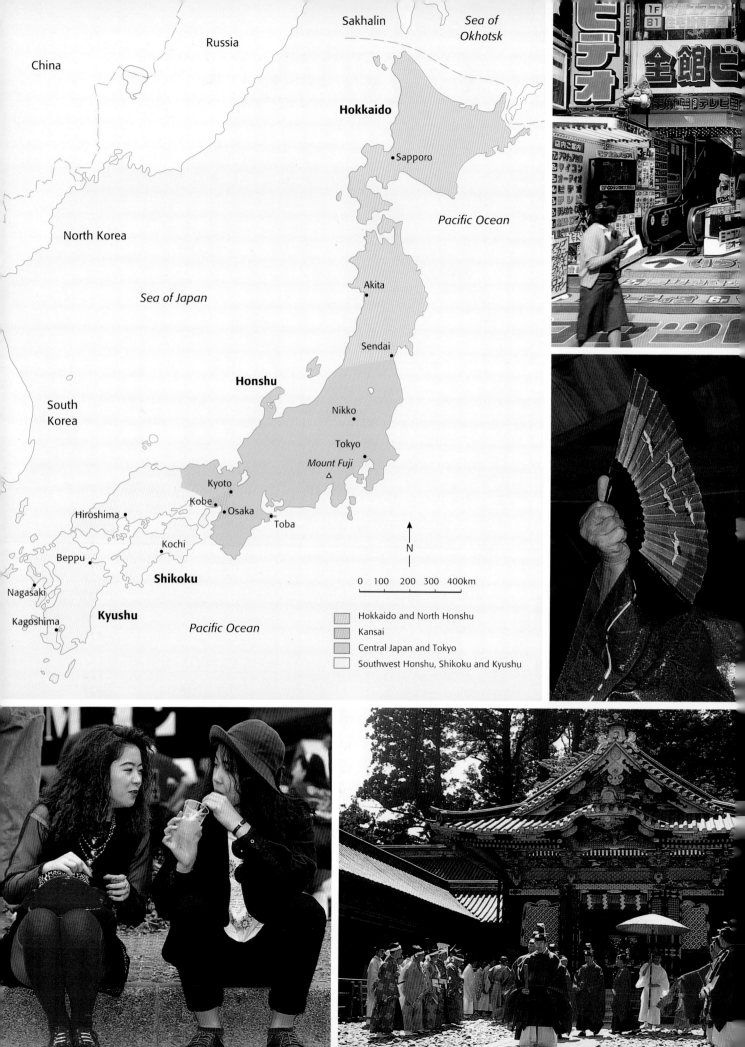

China

Russia

Sakhalin

Sea of Okhotsk

North Korea

Hokkaido

• Sapporo

Pacific Ocean

Sea of Japan

Honshu

Akita

South
Korea

Sendai

Nikko

Tokyo

Mount Fuji
△

Kyoto

Kobe

Osaka

Hiroshima

Toba

Kochi

Beppu

Shikoku

Nagasaki

Kyushu

Pacific Ocean

Kagoshima

N

0 100 200 300 400km

Hokkaido and North Honshu
Kansai
Central Japan and Tokyo
Southwest Honshu, Shikoku and Kyushu

CONTENTS

JAPAN: LAND OF THE RISING SUN

J Japan, the Land of the Rising Sun, is a country full of fascinating contradictions. Ancient temples and shrines, enchanting parks, and rustic ceremonial teahouses nestle between vast skyscrapers covered in garish billboards. Science and culture sit happily hand in hand in this most

technologically innovative of nations, in which the age-old arts of the tea ceremony, flower arranging, theater, calligraphy, and landscape gardening still thrive.

The same contrasts between the traditional and the modern – displayed vividly in many aspects of daily Japanese life – also apply to the preparation and presentation of food. Even though fast food is increasing in popularity in Japan's larger cities, the ancient culinary traditions are lovingly preserved. An integral aspect of these traditions is in the respect given to all types of food, which in times gone by was seen as a gift from the gods.

The visual appeal of food is another very important consideration, for the Japanese demand that a meal – and all that accompanies it – should be a feast for the eyes as well as for the stomach. Whether you patronize a small snack-bar for a quick bite, or are fortunate enough to be invited to share a festive family meal, you will see all around you proof of the time and effort devoted to the choice of ingredients, painstaking preparation, and the decoration of the food and table.

There is no strict order to the menu in Japan, the keyword being variety, for cooks take great pride in the fact that neither the ingredients nor the methods of preparation are repeated in any one meal. The dishes on which the food is served always vary in design and are usually selected to suit the time of year, thus underlining the Japanese belief in human beings' closeness to nature. In

spring, for example, pale, delicate porcelain, or glass bowls and plates will be used, while a winter repast is served on heavier, darker colored ceramic tableware. The ingredients should always be as fresh as possible, and of the highest quality. Seasonings are used sparingly, so that the food tastes natural and unadulterated.

This book is designed to give you an insight into the fascinating land of Japan and its refined yet simple cuisine. The first chapter introduces you to the country and its people, its festivals, traditions, and local culinary specialties. This is followed by seven sections of authentic recipes, each illustrated in color. Variations, short notes, and product information boxes complement the recipes; and clear, step-by-step photographs show some of the more complicated techniques. The book is rounded off with a glossary of some of the less familiar terms and ingredients and a selection of Suggested Menus to help you to plan dishes for anything from a simple supper to a more elaborate dinner party. Bear in mind that the quantities given in the recipes, including those for entrées, are calculated for Japanese servings, which may seem rather small compared with Western portions.

We hope that you will have fun preparing these dishes in your own home, and treating your family and friends to an authentic Japanese meal. So, *itadakimasu!* – as the Japanese say before beginning a meal and enjoy the food of Japan.

CEREMONY AND TRADITION

Japan consists of four main islands, Hokkaido, Honshu, Shiko, and Kyushu, as well as more than 4,000 smaller island, which lie off the coast of Siberia in the north Pacific. Extending from north to south in a length arc, the archipelago is influenced by almost all of the earth's different climatic zones. In winter, the most northerly of the main islands, Hokkaido, is bitterly cold, while the islands below Kyushu are subtropical. The regions between Tokyo, on Honshu, and northern Kyushu, enjoy a temperate climate. Winters are not too cold, while the summers are not unbearably hot. Much of Japan is very mountainous, so the residential and industrial zones are all situated mainly along the coasts or in the valleys. As a consequence, the country's population is crammed into only 20 percent of the landmass.

For centuries, this island nation was largely isolated from the rest of the world, so its people became accustomed to living only on the foods they could forage or grow themselves. The sea provided them with rich supplies of fish, seafood and seaweed, while the fertile soil furnished rice, which had been cultivated on the land since time immemorial. Even today, it is this patchwork of rice fields, large and small, which lends the Japanese landscape its unique character. The importance of rice in the Japanese diet is neatly illustrated by the word *gohan*, which means both "rice" and "meal." For the Japanese, a meal without rice is an unthinkable prospect.

Japan's landscape is dominated by spectacular mountain ranges. The fertile plains on which cereals, soy beans, potatoes, vegetables, fruit, and rice are grown account for only 15 percent of the land surface. There is scant room, too, for grazing land. As a result, cattle-rearing, which was only introduced in the early 19th century, plays a minor role in the economy, and many areas of the country have to rely on supplies of imported meat.

In the late 6th century A.D., Buddhism was introduced to Japan and with it came a prohibition on the hunting and killing of animals. It is thanks to the Buddhist tradition that the Japanese developed their wide range of soybean products – miso (soybean paste), soy sauce, and tofu (soybean curd) – all invented to compensate for the lack of meat in the diet. And there were other benefits, too, for at the same time a distinctive and delicious range of vegetable dishes was created.

Along with rice, the country's most important food, and one of the glories of its cuisine, fish is a staple of the Japanese diet. Between 100 and 150 different types are on sale daily at Japan's largest fish market in Tokyo.

Hokkaido and the North

The north of Japan is one of the least known regions of the country. One of the reasons for this apparent neglect may be that, compared with other areas, such as central Japan, it has fewer great art treasures with which to attract the tourists. Another reason, of course, may be the climate, for in winter the snow lies several feet deep and the air is cold and icy. Even so, it is well worth making a detour from the usual tourist trail to explore this area, for it has much to offer.

In the north, there is no point in seeking the highly industrialized, heavily populated landscape that typifies Japan in the popular imagination, for the area is very rural, much of it is still a wilderness. The northernmost island of Hokkaido, which comprises about 20 percent of the country's land surface, is home to only 5 percent of its population. To draw a pertinent comparison, in Tokyo there are more than 10,000 inhabitants per square mile; in Hokkaido, a similar sized area contains fewer than 70 people.

Since there is no industry in the north, the countryside remains largely unspoiled and undeveloped, with an appealing combination of clear mountain lakes and lush woodlands in its national parks, and sweeping fields and pastures.

Traditions long forgotten in the big cities still survive in the north. The most obvious examples are the regional festivals (*matsuri*), celebrated in both winter and summer. During the cold season, many village-dwellers drive away the evil spirits of winter with time-honored rituals involving riotous feasting and lots of warming rice wine. In February, many Japanese go to Sapporo, the capital of Hokkaido, for Yuki-matsuri, the famous Snow Festival. For the occasion, Odiri, the wide boulevard running through the city center, is filled with a fabulous display of huge snow sculptures – castles, scenes from fairy tales, animals, even whole cities – their lifespan sadly all too short.

An underwater tunnel links Hokkaido with Honshu, the largest of Japan's four main islands. The north, which consists of six prefectures – Aomori, Akita, Iwate, Miyagi, Yamagata, and Fukushima – is renowned for its scenic beauty. Here, the festivals take place in the warm month of August. They include the Hanagasa festival in Yamagata and the Kanto festival in Akita, the purpose of which is to bring about a good harvest in the fall.

At the Nebuta festival in Aomori, floats bearing huge papier-mâchè figures – some of them quite terrifying-looking – parade through the town. According to legend, the ceremony has its origins in a military ploy. During a battle against the Ainu, the mysterious ancient inhabitants of the north, a Japanese commander used gigantic papier-mâchè effigies to scare the enemy, attacking them as they retreated. The ruse appears to have worked, for the Ainu fled north in fright to Hokkaido, where they took refuge and eventually settled. Today, their descendants number around 16,000. They were once a tribe of fishermen and hunters but most of them now make their living from the land.

Clouds of steam billow from the Lo-san volcano in Akan national park. Japan has dozens of such active volcanoes, and many more which remain dormant.

Gleaming white in the sunshine, this massive statue of a goddess dominates the lakeside skyline close to the town of Aizu-Wakamatsu.

An Ainu man eyes the camera warily. Some 16,000 Ainu, descendants of Japan's aboriginal inhabitants, now live on Hokkaido; they occupy about a hundred villages grouped in the south and east of the island.

Northern Honshu has a cool climate, suitable for cultivating such crops as wheat, potatoes, buckwheat, rice, and fruits. Yamagata, on the west coast, is famous for its delicious apples and also produces 75 percent of Japan's cherry crop. The buckwheat grown here is used to make the popular soba noodles.

One Iwate specialty worth sampling is *wanko-soba*. Some noodles – just enough of them to slurp down in one mouthful – are placed in a bowl, together with a little cold broth and a variety of additional ingredients such as chopped chicken in a spicy sweet sauce, nori seaweed, green onions (scallions), walnuts, and/or tunafish. When you have finished the first helping, the waitress –

who is standing behind you while you eat – immediately replaces the empty bowl with a full one, and so on until you have had your fill. Incidentally, the phrase "slurp down" is an appropriate one, for in Japan it is considered the height of good manners to make a lot of noise when eating noodles!

Rice is also grown on the large, neat farms of Hokkaido where, owing to the development of hardy rice varieties, the annual yield is almost as high as in the southern islands. In addition, Hokkaido's farmers are Japan's leading producers of milk and other dairy products. The island is also renowned for *kombu* – a type of seaweed harvested from the surrounding seas.

Kansai

To travel to the historic region of Kansai is to take a journey back into Japanese history. This small, densely populated region, lying between the cities of Kobe, Osaka, and Kyoto, has a wealth of ancient art treasures. According to legend, the first capital of the island kingdom was founded by Emperor Jimmu in the 7th century B.C. in the countryside south of Kyoto. Until the 8th century A.D., the court would move to a new royal city following the death of the current ruler. Before Nara became the first permanent capital in 710, it was considered that a city in which a ruler had died was defiled. Only when Buddhism began to gain a foothold in Japan did this belief wane.

Japan's indigenous religion, before the first monks brought the teachings of Buddhism across from Korea in the late 6th century, was Shinto. It was originally a nameless creed, but was subsequently given the name Shinto, meaning "Way of the Gods" to avoid confusion with the new religion. Central to the rituals of Shinto, which has survived virtually unchanged to the present day, are the gods and spirits of nature known as *kami*. These are shadowy manifestations of power rather than individual, distinct personalities and are associated with particular places, at which shrines are erected in their honor. Though *kami* inhabit their own world, they have the ability to possess and influence humans, and to work through them.

It took nearly a century for Buddhism to become established in Japan. It was introduced as the official religion in the 7th century by Crown Prince Shotoko Taish, who founded a number of temples, including Horyu-ji, five miles south of Nara. Surrounded by wooded hills, and dotted with many gardens and ponds, Nara is one of Japan's loveliest cities, and home to some of its most ancient and historically important buildings. One such site is the Kasuga Shrine, one of Japan's oldest Shinto shrines. It was founded in 768 and is dedicated to mythological Japanese war heroes and other illustrious ancestors.

The temple of Horyu-ji (mentioned above) is the world's oldest existing wooden building, and the largest temple in east Asia to have survived in its original condition. The carpenters who worked on its construction around A.D. 600 used wood from hinoki trees – a kind of cedar – in the firm belief that it would last 2,000 years.

Nara served as the imperial headquarters for only a hundred years. In 784, Emperor Kanmu moved the court to Heian-kyo (later be renamed Kyoto) in order to be as far removed as possible from the Buddhist temple at Nara. The monks were beginning to interfere in state affairs and to pose a threat to the ruling dynasty. Kyoto

Buddhist monks share a joke at Kyoto's Daigo-ji temple. Followers of the religion are renowned for their cheerful disposition.

Craggy stones contrast with carefully raked gravel in this Zen stone garden in Kyoto. The pure shapes are thought to induce spiritual serenity.

remained the cultural, religious, and, with some interruption, political center of Japan for over a thousand years.

Kyoto still enchants visitors with its over 1,500 Buddhist temples, monasteries, and gardens, around 400 Shinto shrines, and a lovely old town. A number of ancient traditions and crafts are preserved in the city, including the tea ceremony, and *ikebana*, the art of flower-arranging. Each temple and shrine holds an annual festival, the most famous of which is the 1,000-year old Gion festival, held at the Yasaka Shrine in mid-July. It is celebrated with a procession of decorated floats, accompanied by costumed revelers.

Kyoto cuisine is strongly influenced by the *kaiseki* style, which involves serving a large number of small, exquisitely presented dishes. Another influence is vegetarian temple cooking (*shojin-ryori*), which was developed by Buddhist

monks. If you are lucky enough to be invited to share such a meal in a temple, do not be deterred by the prospect that, for religious reasons, it will contain no meat, fish, or eggs, for it is a delicious style of cooking, which will appeal to even the most avowed meat-eater.

A stark contrast to the reverent, somewhat conservative atmosphere of Kyoto is provided by the lively port of Osaka, whose history is even more ancient than Kyoto's (archeological excavations have revealed evidence of early imperial palaces). Northwest of Osaka lies the international port of Kobe, which is principally famous for its meat. The beef cattle here are reared on a special diet, which results in the meat being marbled with fat, and therefore unusually tender. The local version of *sukiyaki*, thin slices of beef simmered in a mixture of soy sauce and sake, is especially delicious.

Tourists gaze in awe at the most famous of Kyoto's 400 shrines, the Heian Shrine, dedicated to Emperor Kanmu, founder of Kyoto.

This moss-covered stone vessel is used for cleansing the mouth and hands before the tea ceremony.

北 杜夫 原作
堀越 真 脚本
杉田成道 演出

楡家の人びと

Central Japan and Tokyo

Central Japan is divided into three districts: Kanto, Chubu, and Hokuriku. Kanto, which in the last hundred years has developed into the country's most highly industrialized and densely populated region, is the location of Japan's highest and most famous mountain. Mount Fuji – known in Japan as Fujiyama or Fuji-san. Symbol of the entire land, which is bisected and dominated by the great mountain ranges that cover more than 80 percent of its terrain, it is revered because of its beautiful snow-capped cone and immense size. Though now extinct, Mount Fuji has made a very significant contribution over the centuries to the improvement in the region's fortunes, for its volcanic ash has transformed the clay soil of the surrounding fields into the highly fertile agricultural land it is today.

The focal point of Kanto is Tokyo. This immense city, capital of Japan since 1868, is one of the world's largest, with between 10 and 25 million inhabitants, depending on whether you include the populations of Kawasaki, Yokohama, and other neighboring towns that belong within the region known as Greater Tokyo.

A fascinating, dynamic metropolis, Tokyo is the industrial, administrative, political, and financial heart of Japan. During its relatively short 400-year history, it has been regularly ravaged by earthquakes, fire, and war, especially the air raids of 1945. Each time the city has been rebuilt in a larger and completely different form. As a consequence, although it has preserved much of its original shape, there are few remaining buildings that predate the World War II.

One of this crowded city's most famous commercial districts is the Ginza, whose streets are packed with stores, cafés, and restaurants and always full of people. Shopping is a favorite Japanese pastime. Many people spend their leisure hours just browsing in the elegant department stores. Even family outings on Sundays can turn into shopping expeditions.

Tokyo is full of life around the clock. Many stores stay open until 8 p.m. and some are open 24 hours a day. As late as 4 o'clock in the morning you can still find a hot meal in the Shinjuku quarter. Shortly afterwards still in the early hours, the day's auctioning begins at the Tsukiji fish market. This market is the largest of its kind in the world and attracts the city's restaurateurs and chefs as well as its fishmongers. The auction of the many types of fish and seafood begins at around 5 a.m. It is a fascinating spectacle, well worth getting up early for. Afterward, you can make your way to one of the many small nearby restaurants for an early breakfast of sushi, or miso soup, rice, vegetables and, of course, fried fish.

Tokyo's most imposing building is the Imperial Palace. Twice a year, on New Year's Day and on the emperor's birthday on 23 December, visitors are permitted to get close enough to catch a glimpse of it. The remainder of the time, a stroll

through the vast grounds is all that is allowed. Not to be missed, either, is the Kannon temple in the district of Asakusa, one of Tokyo's oldest Buddhist buildings. Its outstanding feature is a huge, five-story pagoda. Another favorite outing is a visit to Ueno Park, an attraction for old and young alike with its lake, temples, and shrines, as well as the Tokyo National Museum. In spring, when the cherry trees for which Japan is so famous are heavy with blossom, the park is frequently full to bursting, every corner occupied with families and groups of workers, their picnics laid out before them.

Kamakura, 30 miles south of Tokyo, is another popular destination. Between 1192 and 1331, it was the seat of government of the feudal shoguns – a line of hereditary military dictators – during which time the emperor remained powerless in Kyoto. Many of Kamakura's temples, and its cast 13th-century bronze of Buddha, are a legacy of the shoguns. The Great Buddha, built in 1253, towers to a height of almost 50 feet; it is one of the largest and most beautiful of its kind in Japan.

Nearby is a beautiful stretch of wild Pacific coastline, whose beaches – collectively known as the "Japanese Riviera" – are a popular tourist attraction. The prefectures of Yamanashi, Nagano, and Gifu, situated in the mountainous heart of Honshu, are jointly known as the "Roof of Japan." Much of their majestic scenery is protected in national parks.

Fall foliage provides the perfect foil for snow-capped mountains near Takayama, in the Japanese Alps.

Beautifully sculpted trees and bushes nestle in the splendid landscaped gardens of Suizen-ji Park, southwest of Kyushu.

Steam billows from a carved and painted dragon's head set among the hot springs in Beppu, northern Kyushu.

The Temperate South

The southwestern arm of Honshu, Japan's main island, is bisected lengthwise by the Chugoku mountain range. On the northern side of the mountains, facing the Sea of Japan, the weather is particularly mild and sunny, even in winter. During the hot summer months, the sandy beaches attract crowds of swimmers and sunbathers. The southern side has a number of important towns, among them Okayama, famous for its beautiful, unglazed pottery, and the busy commercial city of Kurashiki, worth a visit for its many interesting old warehouses. Further west is the port of Hiroshima, largely destroyed in 1945 by the first atomic bomb to be dropped in warfare; a museum here commemorates the tragedy, which cost the lives of more than 75,000 people.

Not far from Hiroshima is the little island of Miyajima, on whose coast stands one of the loveliest and most renowned shrines in Japan. Built in 811, the Itsukushima Shrine, whose buildings are linked by long, red-painted corridors, is dedicated to three Shinto goddesses. Even more famous than the shrine is its red, camphor-wood shrine gate, or *torii*. Standing in the shallow waters of the bay, about 530 feet offshore, it has become one of the symbols of Japan.

For travelers to South Korea, the ferry leaves daily from the port of Shimonoseki, situated at the extreme western point of Honshu. From here, you can also get to the fourth main island, Kyushu, via a bridge or subway train. By far the most pleasant way to make the trip across, however, is by boat, which provides an ideal opportunity to appreciate the beauty of the Inland Sea, the 312-mile-wide stretch of water lying between Honshu, Shikoku, and Kyushu. Only a few miles wide in places, it is dotted with countless little oddly shaped islands. The center of the Inland Sea is now a nature reserve.

Shikoku, the smallest of the four main islands, does not feature prominently in mainstream tourist itineraries. The majority of its Japanese visitors come as pilgrims, for it was on this island in 744 that Kobo Daishi, founder of the Shingon Buddhist sect, was born. Japan's most famous pilgrimage route leads through 88 temples, all of them dedicated to Daishi. There are some other charming attractions on offer, however, many of them still relatively tourist-free. They include the famous garden at Takamatsu, with its many ponds and tea pavilions, the pleasant paths through the mountains and forests, and the museum village displaying ancient farmhouses and teahouses. Kochi, on the Pacific coast, is famed for its exquisite fish dishes, while Kagawa, in the north, is known for its homemade udon noodles.

The Volcanoes of Kyushu

Much of Kyushu's north coast has been taken over by industry. By contrast, in the warm and humid underdeveloped south, the emphasis is on agriculture. Here, in the fertile volcanic soil, citrus fruits and a wide variety of vegetables flourish. But the focal point of Kyushu is its mountainous heart; Japan has around 200 volcanoes, the most active

of which are situated here. The most restless of them all is Mount Sakurajima, overlooking the town of Kagoshima; it periodically hurls clouds of black ash and chunks of lava into the air. As protection against a sudden volcanic bombardment, concrete shelters are provided at intervals along the coast road – a grim warning for the passing tourist of the powder keg on which Kyushu's inhabitants live. However, the people of the south have a very relaxed attitude toward the threat of eruption, which they have learned to live with.

The largest volcanic crater on earth is to be found in Aso National Park. It covers approximately 2187 square miles

and is inhabited by about 70,000 people, who live in little towns and villages clustered in the crater.

The cosmopolitan city of Nagasaki lies in western Kyushu. This ancient center of commerce (which suffered the same atomic catastrophe as Hiroshima) was engaged in foreign trade during the 250 years of Japan's isolation. Between the 17th and 19th centuries, business with China and Holland boomed. As a result, there are clearly discernible foreign influences on the regional cuisine. Flavors, for example, are generally much sweeter than in other parts of Japan. *Nori*, a particularly delicious type of seaweed, is grown in the warm waters around Kyushu. Cultivated under careful supervision, it is harvested in winter – either by hand or with suction pumps – and processed. Dried *nori* is supplied to towns and cities throughout Japan and is highly popular as a sushi wrapping.

Two martial arts experts demonstrate the dramatic art of kendo – dueling with bamboo staves – which was practiced by the samurai.

Rising from the shallow waters off Miyajima Island, this camphor-wood gate has become the symbol of Japan.

Brilliant, carp-shaped cloth flags flutter in the wind before the stunning snow-capped cone of Mount Fuji. The flags are traditionally hoisted by families on Boys' Day, in honor of their sons.

Festivals and Present-Giving

If you have always believed the Japanese to be a polite and reserved people, you really should attend a Shinto festival. Many Shinto shrines and Buddhist temples organize a major annual festival in honor of a god or spirit, and such occasions are famous for their riotous dancing and drumming and for the copious amounts of rice wine that are consumed. During the celebrations, relays of men and women run through the streets, carrying or pulling the local *kami* (god) behind them in its heavy and unwieldy *mikoshi*, or ornamental shrine. The perspiring bearers are accompanied by drummers, people in costume and, of course, crowds of excited onlookers.

Most Japanese festivals have a very long history, and many of them date back centuries. The majority involve prayer or thanksgiving. Prayers may be offered for a good harvest, or thanks given for the birth of healthy children.

Japan has a lot of national holidays, some of which have been introduced to compensate for the reluctance among Japanese workers to take paid leave. Most firms and offices close down for at least the first three days of the New Year, when people visit temples and meet up with family and friends. The most important festival takes place on New Year's Day itself. Just before midnight on December 31, the old year is seen out with a dish of *soba*, the long buckwheat noodles that traditionally symbolize longevity.

Many of Japan's festivals relate to specific stages in a person's lifetime. For example, September 15 is Respect for the Aged Day, when elderly people are given special attention. The Doll Festival, on March 3, is a celebration for

all little girls, on which they are taught to pray for a happy marriage when the time is right. The day's accompanying festival is marked, like many such occasions, by the sharing of a special dish or drink, in this case *shirozake*, a mixture of sweet rice and malt wine. Boy's Day, which falls on May 5, is celebrated by the hoisting of flags in the shape of a carp, symbol of strength and masculinity. The food that is enjoyed on this day includes *kashiwamochi*, little rice cakes filled with sweet bean paste. On every children's festival it is customary for families to visit the shrines to pray for a happy future for their offspring.

Both Boy's Day and Constitution Day, on May 3 form part of the so-called "Golden Week," a cluster of public holidays that begins on April 29 (birthday of former Emperor Hirohito) with a celebration of the beauties of

nature. It is not a good idea to try to travel around Japan during Golden Week, for the whole of the country is on the move and it becomes virtually impossible to find a spare seat on a train or boat. The same applies around August 15, the Buddhist equivalent of All Saints' Day. During this period, so it is widely believed, the spirits of the dead come back to spend time with their families, who traditionally come together to greet the spirits.

Another dearly held custom in Japan is the giving of presents. In addition to marking familiar occasions such as birthdays or weddings, the many feast days provide regular – and frequent – opportunities for the offering of a gift to family, friends, and colleagues. The classic gift seasons are *O-chugen* (in July) and *O-seibo* (in December); twice a year, workers give presents to their colleagues, superiors, and customers. Almost as important as the present itself is its obligatory elaborate and attractive wrapping, which is regarded as a sign of respect for the recipient.

Indeed, the value of the present is often less important that the manner in which it is presented. Gifts often consist of something edible – particularly in mid-summer and at New Year – and may comprise a perfect bowl of strawberries or a particularly fine melon. Candies, too, are popular, as are colored gelatin desserts or small, filled cakes, each one beautifully presented in its own individual packaging, like an exquisite jewel. If you are welcomed to stay as a guest in somebody's house in Japan, you should always take with you a few souvenirs typical of your homeland, for presentation to your hosts.

Male and female bearers at a Shinto festival cheerfully carry a heavy shrine through the streets of Tokyo's Harajuku district

Dressed in traditional costume, children in Akita celebrate the snow festival.

On Sundays in Tokyo, the fashionable meeting place for the young is Yoyogi Park.

Their heads bowed, children in Osaka are addressed by their headmaster. Discipline and a sense of community are viewed as an essential part of a child's education.

The Japanese Family

Slowly, but perceptibly, Japanese society is beginning to change. On average, people are marrying later, one of the reasons being that many young women today are choosing to go on to higher education and to work for a while before settling down. At the same time, fewer young men are willing to devote their working lives to one firm, which has altered working patterns and fostered greater competition for jobs.

Japanese women usually marry around the age of 24, and men by age 28 at the latest. Those who cannot find a suitable partner for themselves are often helped by parents, friends, and well-meaning acquaintances, who act as go-betweens for prospective partners. And sometimes firms, too will organize an arranged meeting – known as an *o-miai* – in order to help a valued employee to tie the knot.

Weddings in Japan are traditionally elaborate affairs, celebrated in luxury surroundings, accompanied by family, friends, acquaintances, colleagues – and even the boss. In present-day Japan, the choice of a Shinto, Buddhist, or Christian marriage ceremony often depends less on the religious affiliations of the bridal pair than on which proceedings will look the most impressive to the guests.

Within marriage, the wife has the main responsibility for the care and upbringing of the children, choosing their kindergarten and schools. The word "housewife" is regarded as a term of respect in Japan, for society places a high value on running a home and raising children. The early years of a child's life are taken very seriously. To outsiders, parents may appear to be very indulgent toward their offspring, who are actually nurtured in a very secure atmosphere, in which they are encouraged to observe and emulate the behavior of their elders and are seldom punished.

A sense of public-spiritedness and consideration for others is instilled from an early age, for Japanese life focuses not so much on the individual as on the group. In contrast, say, to an American upbringing, where energy is largely devoted to the development of the image of the individual, in Japan it is directed toward the team – whether the family, school, company, club, or circle of friends. The teaching of this philosophy continues throughout kindergarten and school and on into the workplace.

Japanese fathers generally work such long hours that they only get to spend time with their children at the weekends. For the majority of men, life has always centered around work and continues to do so. At one time, a Japanese man "belonged" to his company from the day

he joined, and it was quite normal for an employee to devote his entire career to the same firm. In return for his commitment, he joined the "corporate community" and was guaranteed good prospects and financial security for the whole of his working life. Even today, young men do not find moving to a new job easy; having been brought up with a strong group ethic, they feel close ties with their earliest employers and have a deeply ingrained sense of company loyalty.

The working day in Japan begins between 8.30 and 9.00 a.m. and usually ends around 6 p.m. For many however, this is not the end of their duties, for it is customary – even when faced with a long homeward journey – to go for a drink or meal with colleagues or clients. For those who live outside Tokyo and commute to work in the city center, this compulsory socializing is followed by a journey of over an hour in very packed trains or through streets that are jammed with traffic.

Many families would never dream of asking their work colleagues or distant acquaintances home for a meal. The main reason for this is that most Japanese live in very small apartments, with tiny kitchens, so they prefer to take their guests out to eat. Meals at home are largely family affair – shared only by relatives or old friends – but this does not mean that any less love or care goes into their preparation.

Usually, there are three meals a day: breakfast, lunch, and dinner. A bowl of rice, and miso soup, form the mainstay of every meal, including breakfast. The other dishes vary according to the time of day. At midday, mothers generally cook only for their children, since husbands seldom work close by. They will occasionally cook dishes from Europe or other parts of Asia, such as a curry or spaghetti, though the food is seasoned with soy sauce in deference to Japanese tastes. Of all the meals of the day, the greatest care is lavished on dinner; if the husband manages to arrive home early enough – though this is rare – the whole family will enjoy it together in leisurely fashion.

Bathers young and old enjoy the hot bath at Ofuro, intended to cleanse the soul rather than the body. Men and women use separate bathhouses, and bathers are required to wash thoroughly before entering the water.

A Brief Style Guide

Japanese cuisine is full of underlying symbolism and ritual. If you take the time to acquire a little knowledge about such traditions as the centuries-old tea ceremony, choosing what to drink, table decoration, and how to handle chopsticks, you will find that it will make your first steps into the world of Japan and its delicious food a fascinating and ultimately very rewarding experience.

Drinks to accompany food
Traditionally, the Japanese drink green tea and sake with their meals. Today, however, ice-cold beer is a popular choice. When you invite guests to share a Japanese meal, you can serve sake, either warm or cold, to begin with. When the rice arrives, you should switch to tea, since sake, being made from fermented rice, is considered an unsuitable accompaniment. In summer the Japanese enjoy cold *mugicha*, a refreshing tea made from toasted barley grains. A courtesy carefully observed in Japan is choosing exactly the right moment to top up your guests' drinks. When the drinks are poured, guests toast each other with the word *kanpai* – cheers!

The tea ceremony
This ancient ritual – still participated in regularly by some two million Japanese – was brought from China to Japan by Zen Buddhist monks around 700 A.D. It traditionally takes place in special rustic teahouses (built of natural materials such as bamboo, wood and paper), set within beautiful temple gardens. the appreciation of the

After measuring out two to three scoops of finely ground tea into a bowl, the tea master pours boiling water over it with a bamboo dipper. The liquid is then gently beaten to a froth with a special bamboo whisk, before being served.

setting, the room's austere decor, and the various utensils used for the tea-making are all essential aspects of the ceremony, which was devised primarily as an aesthetic and spiritual experience rather than a culinary one.

Before guests enter the teahouse they must first rinse the mouth and hands in the fresh spring water contained in a stone vessel placed at the edge of the path before the entrance. The tea itself – a bitter, finely ground green tea known as *match* – is carefully prepared by the tea master in accordance with a strictly prescribed ritual. He pours the tea into a bowl and whisks it with a bamboo whisk. The frothy tea is then served to each of the participants in turn, beginning with the guest of honor. It is drunk very slowly and with great reverence.

During the first stages of the cere-mony – which can last several hours if it incorporates a meal (*kaiseki*) – small dishes of food are passed as refresh-ment. Candies are traditionally served to counteract the bitter taste of the tea.

How to handle chopsticks

As anyone who has tried using a pair of chopsticks for the first time knows, it takes quite a bit of practice before you feel confident eating with them in public! Chopsticks are supplied at and used throughout every meal in Japan. When not in use, they should be placed on the little chopstick rest. If there is no rest to hand, simply lay them across a shallow bowl, such as a bowl containing soy sauce.

There are two strict taboos relating to the use of chopsticks. Firstly, you should never stick them into the rice, and, secondly, food should never be passed from one set of chopsticks to another. Both of these actions are associated with funerary rituals, and will cause great offense to a Japanese person. It is also impolite, even during a lively discussion, to point at a person or object with your chopsticks.

If you wish to help yourself to rice or other food from a communal serving dish, simply turn the chopsticks round and use the ends that have not been near your mouth. When eating with chopsticks, it is correct to hold your bowl at about chest level, to make it easier to lift the food to the mouth. If you are preparing Japanese food, it is a good idea to make sure that all the ingredients are cut into bite-sized pieces so that they can more easily be picked up with chopsticks. It is acceptable to lift large chunks to your mouth and to bite off smaller pieces.

Soup is always drunk straight from the bowl, and the solid ingredients tackled with chopsticks. An exception is made for fruit or gelatin dessert, which can be eaten with a decorative wooden toothpick or a fork, and ice cream, for which a spoon is used.

Table settings are kept simple, in order not to detract in any way from the beautifully presented and carefully balanced food, and any decorations must be used sparingly. Bare twigs or a few flowers, in a plain vase, are a favorite choice. *Ikebana*, the popular Japanese art of flower arranging, is never employed for table decoration.

In the austere setting which the occasion demands, a tea master and her daughter, both wearing traditional kimonos, participate in the tea ceremony.

Holding her bowl of rice at the correct chest-level height, a young woman deftly picks up a mouthful of food.

The traditional and the modern meet in a lively fast-food restaurant in Tokyo's Harajuku district. Eating out is an immensely popular pastime in Japan, which has restaurants to cater for every possible taste and budget.

Japanese Restaurants

Eating out plays an important part in the business and social life of the Japanese. For many "company men," a meal with colleagues or clients in a smart restaurant is the customary end to the working day, and is seen not as an indulgence but as a necessity, and as an indication of status. Indeed, restaurant entertaining is practically essential to the conclusion of any business deal, large or small.

As a consequence, Japan has a wide and thriving variety of bars and restaurants, many of which specialize in one type of food, for example sushi, or noodles. If you have a problem describing what you want, you'll find that most restaurants conveniently display very realistic, though gaudy, plastic replicas of their dishes in their display window. Your waiter or waitress will always be happy to come with you so that you can indicate your choice. Meals are usually paid for at the till as you leave, and it is not considered necessary to leave a tip.

One popular culinary specialty is bento-box meals. A bento box is a small lunch box, with separate compartments for rice, fish, meat, and vegetables. Most restaurants offer a delivery service to homes and offices. Bento boxes are also sold at theaters, railroad stations, and on trains.

Specialty restaurants

At midday, Japanese office workers usually go to a noodle restaurant to eat *soba* or *udon* dishes. After work, the bars known as *nomi-ya* are popular haunts. Here rice wine, beer, or whisky is the customary tipple, accompanied by various small snacks.

Delicious, charcoal-grilled foods are the specialty of the popular *yakitori-ya*. In these restaurants, little pieces of chicken, variety meats, vegetables, or fish are threaded onto bamboo skewers and dipped in a variety of sauces, or simply salted, before being quickly grilled over a charcoal fire.

Tempura is a favorite Japanese cooking method. Everything on the menu of a tempura restaurant – small pieces of fish, shrimp, and vegetables are dipped in a light batter and deep-fried. Restaurants known as *tonkatsu-ya* offer breaded pork chops (*tonkatsu*) with a special sauce, and at teppanyaki restaurants food is cooked on a griddle in front of the customer.

O-konomiyaki restaurants specialize in a kind of pancake with other ingredients such as vegetables and seafood; customers create their own pancakes on a hotplate placed on the table. Other restaurants specialize in *sukiyaki* – Japanese meat fondue – eel dishes, tofu or vegetarian dishes.

Shojin-ryori, the Buddhist temple restaurants, are especially renowned for their meat-free fare. However, the most famous of Japanese restaurants are sushi restaurants. At first, Americans might find these pieces of raw fish served on vinegar-flavored rice a somewhat strange experience, but they will soon be converted. There are many varieties of these tasty and decorative tidbits which are dipped in soy sauce before eating. Each town and region in Japan has its own special sushi dish. Today, sushi is renowned throughout the world.

Kaiseki restaurants

These are regarded as the finest of the specialty restaurants for their cuisine is rooted in the ancient tea ceremony. The meal is eaten in the setting of an austere room, carpeted with *tatami*, rice-straw matting, and dinners are obliged to remove their shoes before entering. The table, at which the diners kneel, is in the center of the room One corner of the room is adorned with a beautiful flower arrangement or work of art, and the guest of honor is placed facing this corner. Many *kaiseki* restaurants only accept recommended customers, and it is always wise to reserve in advance. The 15 or more courses that are traditionally served comprise a variety of small delicacies.

One of the great Japanese culinary delicacies is *fugu* (globefish), served in *kaiseki* and special fugu restaurants. The liver and ovaries of this fish, which is found only in the Pacific, contain a deadly poison for which there is no

The immaculate coiffure, white make-up, and red lipstick of this geisha girl are all traditional hallmarks of her profession, one that takes many years of study to master.

known antidote. Only licensed cooks are allowed to prepare this dish, which is regarded as a luxury and priced accordingly.

In the smoky atmosphere of a jolly little snack bar, Japanese office workers enjoy a drink before setting out on the long and often arduous journey home.

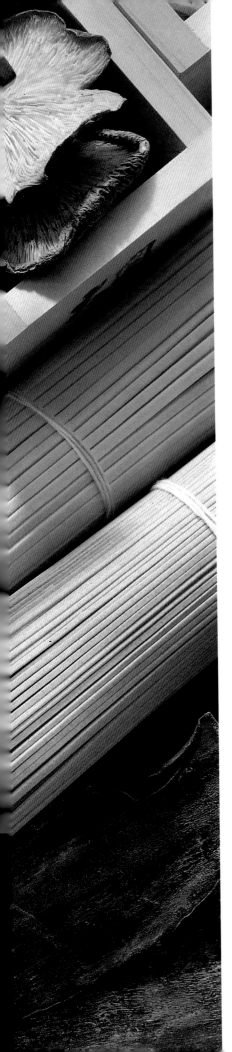

SOUPS

Soups form part of every meal in Japan, whatever the time of day. They are not served as a first course as they are in the United States, but as a side dish or in-between courses, depending on the menu.

There are two basic types of soups, clear soups and miso soups. The best-known clear soup is *dashi*, a delicate, fat-free broth made from water, *kombu* (a type of seaweed) and dried, flaked *bonito*. *Dashi* is the basic ingredient of a great many Japanese dishes, as well as other soups, among them the famous *misoshiru*. Miso soups are clear soups flavored with white or red soybean paste, which gives them their rich flavor and thicker consistency. They are a popular breakfast food in Japan.

Delicately flavored dishes are always accompanied by a clear soup, traditionally brought to a table in a lidded lacquered wood bowl called an *o-wan*. More substantial main-course soups – such as a lunch-time noodle soup – are generally served in large earthenware or porcelain bowls. The solid ingredients of a soup are always eaten first with chopsticks, then the broth is drunk. Do not worry if this leads to some noisy eating – in Japan, slurping is positively encouraged when consuming soup, and is regarded as a sign of good breeding.

The recipes in this chapter indicate whether the soup is intended as a entrée or a side dish.

Basic Soup Broth (Dashi 1)

Simple • Basic recipe **Ichiban dashi 1**

Makes 3½ cups (Serves 4)

**6-in. square sheetkombu seaweed
(see page 31)
3 heaping tbsp. hanakatsuo
(flaked, dried bonito)**

Preparation time: 15 minutes

26 cal. per serving

1 Carefully wipe the seaweed with a cloth (*above*); on no account wash it. Place the seaweed in a saucepan with 3½ cups water and bring slowly to a boil, uncovered, over medium heat. As soon as the water begins to boil, lift the seaweed out of the saucepan, using a slotted spoon. Return the flavored water to a boil.

2 Add the hanakatsuo to the boiling water in the saucepan (*above*) and bring back to a boil.

3 Wait for about 1 minute, until the hanakatsuo sinks to the bottom of the pan, then carefully strain the broth

through a cloth (bottom, left). Reserve the seaweed and the hanakatsuo for making dashi 2 (see *below*).

Variation: Dashi 2 (Niban dashi)
This variation of Japanese dashi takes about 30 minutes. Place the seaweed and hanakatsuo from the recipe above in a saucepan with an additional 3 tsp. hanakatsuo and 5 cups water, and bring to a boil. Remove the seaweed. Boil the broth until reduced by a third, then strain through a cloth.

Note: Dashi 1 is the basis of many delicately-flavored soups and sauces. Dashi 2 has a stronger taste and is used for making oven-baked dishes, fish dishes, and miso soups. The broth will keep in the refrigerator for about two days. Traditionally, dashi 2 cannot be prepared without dashi , so for any recipe calling for dashi 2, you must first make dashi 1. However, both kinds of dashi can be made in large quantities and frozen in batches.
When time is short, or you only need a small quantity, you can use instant dashi in powdered form, available from specialty food stores. Simply mix it with boiling water.

Tofu and Wakame Soup

Easy • Entrée   **Tofu to wakamejiru**   ***Serves 4***

4 small pieces wakame seaweed, each about 2 inches square (see opposite)
½ cup fresh, or vacuum-packed, firm tofu (see page 48)
3 ½ cups Dashi 1 (see page 28)
2 tbsp. Japanese soy sauce

Preparation time: 15 minutes (plus 15 minutes for making the dashi)

50 cal. per serving

1 Soak the seaweed in cold water for about 3 minutes

2 Dip the tofu briefly in a bowl of cold water, drain, then cut into ½ in. dice.

3 Pour the dashi into a saucepan and bring to boil, uncovered. Stir in the soy sauce and add the tofu. Remove the pan from the heat.

4 Squeeze the seaweed thoroughly by hand and add it to the soup. Serve in individual bowls.

Variation: Instead of diced tofu, you can use shrimp. Cook 4 peeled and deveined medium-sized shrimp in boiling water for 2 minutes. prepare the seaweed and dashi as described above. Place the seaweed and shrimp in the soup bowls and pour the dashi on top.

Note: The combination of tofu and wakame is a favorite with many Japanese families. You can vary the soup ingredients according to taste. For example, it is very good with abura-age (deep-fried tofu, sold ready-prepared in specialty food stores), potatoes, daikon (Japanese white radish), mushrooms, or green onions (scallions).
Never use more than two or three different ingredients, or you will mask their distinctive flavors.

Seaweed

Seaweed – or marine algae, to give its correct scientific name – plays a major role in Japanese cuisine. Every year some 300,000 tons of it are consumed. As well as enhancing the flavor of other foods, seaweed is a rich source of minerals and vitamins. The good health of the Japanese, despite their limited consumption of foods considered essential in most Western diets, such as milk, eggs, and meat, may well be due to the high percentage of these calorie-free sea vegetables – as well as fish – in their daily diet.

Four main varieties of seaweed are used in Japanese cuisine: kombu, hijiki, wakame and nori. All are found wild in the seas off the coast of Japan, where they are also to some extent cultivated and farmed, prior to harvesting and processing.

Kombu (also known as konbu or "kelp" in English) comes in long brown strips up to 20 feet long in some varieties. The mild flavor is good in broths and soups. *Hijiki* resembles long, black tea leaves. It needs to be soaked for about 2 hours before use and, when cooked, increases in volume fivefold. It is used principally in soups and salads. *Wakame*, like *kombu*, is a brown seaweed, with long, thin fronds. It is added to miso soups and needs short soaking. It is also good in salads. *Nori*, or laver, is pressed into wafer-thin sheets that are shiny dark brown or dark green. It is used for wrapping sushi rolls, or cut into strips for adding to rice. It may be toasted to bring out the flavor.

In the U.S., dried seaweed is sold in specialty and health-food stores.

Clear Soup with Fish Balls

Easy • Entrée **Suimono**   *Serves 4*

1½ cups dashi (see page 28)
1½ tsp. salt
1 tsp. Japanese soy sauce
5 chives
½ cup surimi (crabsticks)
1 egg white
juice of ½ lemon

Preparation time: 20 minutes
(plus 15 minutes for making the
dashi)

45 cal. per serving

1 Pour the dashi into a saucepan and heat through, uncovered, over high heat. Do not allow the soup to boil. Season with 1 tsp. of the salt and the soy sauce.

2 Meanwhile, wash the chives, shake dry, and chop or snip diagonally into small pieces.

3 Finely chop the fish and place in a bowl. Add the remaining salt and stir with a fork until it becomes sticky.

4 Stir in the egg white and knead the mixture to an even-textured dough.

Press the dough through a sieve and with damp hands, shape it into walnut-sized balls or oval shapes.

5 Bring a saucepan of water to a boil, then add the fish balls and cook, uncovered, over medium heat for about 3 minutes.

6 Divide the fish balls between four individual soup bowls and pour the soup over them. Sprinkle with chives and add a squeeze of lemon juice.

Note: Leftover cooked fish can be used to make these fish balls.

Clam Soup

Simple • Entrée **Ushiojuri**   *Serves 4*

12 small clams (about 1 in. in
diameter)
salt
2 in. square piecekombu
seaweed (see page 31)
4 tbsp. sake (Japanese rice wine)
2 tsp. Japanese soy sauce
sansho (Japanese pepper)
leaves
(see Note) or
a 1-in. slice fresh ginger root
for garnish

Preparation time: 20 minutes
(plus 3 hours for soaking the clams)

1 Soak the clams in plenty of salted water for at least 3 hours to remove any sand and grit. scrub the shells thoroughly and discard any open ones.

2 Briefly wipe the seaweed with a damp cloth, but do not rinse. Transfer the clams to a saucepan with 3½ cups water, the seaweed, and sake, and heat through. Remove the seaweed just before the water reaches boiling point. Cook the soup for a further 2 minutes, or until the clams open.

3 Remove the clams and discard any unopened ones. Then strain the soup through a cloth and stir in the soy sauce.

4 Transfer the clams to four soup bowls and top up with the soup. Wash the pepper leaves, shake dry, and use to garnish the soup. If you are using fresh ginger, cut the slice lengthwise into thin matchsticks and sprinkle them over the soup. Serve with rice.

Note: Fresh Japanese pepper leaves are only available from Japanese food stores since they are only used in this dish for their attractive appearance and not for flavor, you can substitute little matchsticks of fresh ginger instead.

Egg Soup

Kakitamajiru   *Serves 4*

1 heaped tbsp. potato starch or
cornstarch
2 eggs
8 mitsuba leaves (Japanese parsley)
or Japanese cress
1 piece fresh ginger root,
about ½ inch
3 ½ cups dashi 1 (see page 28)
2 tsp. sake (Japanese rice wine)

*Preparation time: 20 minutes
(plus 15 minutes for making the
dashi)*

40 cal. per serving

1 Dissolve the potato starch in 1 ½ tbsp. cold water. Whisk the eggs thoroughly in a bowl. Wash and coarsely chop the mitsuba leaves. Peel and finely grate the ginger to extract the juice.

2 Bring the dashi to a boil in an uncovered saucepan. Reduce the heat, then stir in the soy sauce and sake.

3 Stir in the potato starch and cook over low heat until the broth begins to thicken, stirring constantly.

4 Bring the soup briefly back to a boil, and slowly add the eggs, stirring constantly. Season the soup with the ginger juice.

5 Pour into individual bowls to serve and garnish with mitsuba leaves.

Variation: Peel and finely dice 3 yams and 1 small carrot. Trim a leek and cut into thin rings. Dice 10 oz. chicken breast and ½ cup konnyaku (see Glossary). Cut ¾ oz. abura-age (deep-fried tofu) into thin strips. Follow Step 1 above, omitting the eggs. Add the vegetables and konnyaku to the dashi and simmer for 20 minutes. Season with soy sauce and sake and thicken with potato starch. Add the abura-age strips and leek rings just before serving.

Vegetable Soup

Zoni

Takes time • Winter dish

Serves 4

4 dried shiitake mushrooms
4 mochi (Japanese rice cakes)
⅔ cup fresh leaf spinach
3 medium carrots
4 oz. boned chicken thighs, with skin
3 cups Dashi 1 (see page 28)
6 tbsp. Japanese soy sauce
salt

Preparation time: 1 hour (plus 3 hours for soaking the mushrooms and 15 minutes for making the dashi)

310 cal. per serving

1 Soak the dried shiitake mushrooms in 1 cup water for about 3 hours, then remove from the water and discard the stalks. Pour the mushroom water through a sieve, and reserve. Preheat the oven to 250 degrees.

2 In a nonstick skillet without fat, toast the rice cakes over medium heat until golden-brown on both sides, but still soft inside. Keep warm in the oven while making the soup.

3 Trim and wash the spinach. Peel and thinly slice the carrots. Cut the boned chicken thighs into 1-in. pieces.

4 Bring a saucepan of water to a boil. Add the carrots and chicken and blanch for about 1 ½ minutes. Remove from the pan and keep warm. Blanch the spinach for about 30 seconds, then rinse in cold water.

5 Bring the dashi, soy sauce, salt, and ⅓ cup of the reserved mushroom water to a boil, uncovered, in a saucepan, then simmer for about 5 minutes over low heat.

6 Place one rice cake and one shiitake mushroom in each of four Japanese soup bowls (o-wan) or other soup bowls. Divide the spinach, carrots, and chicken between the bowls and pour in the soup. Serve at once.

Note: During New Year celebrations, from January 1st to the 3rd, it is traditional to serve soup instead of rice.

Miso Soup with Vegetables

Easy • Entrée **Nameko to daikon-oroshi no misoshiru** *Serves 4*

3 oz. daikon (Japanese white radish)
6 tbsp. canned nameko mushrooms or fresh shiitake mushrooms
3 ½ cups dashi 2 (see page 28)
5 tbsp. miso (soybean paste see page 38)
4 chives (optional)

Preparation time: 15 minutes (plus 30 minutes for preparing the dashi)

95 cal. per serving

1 Peel the daikon and slice it thinly with a cucumber slicer and drain in a sieve. Place the canned mushrooms in a colander and briefly rinse them to make them less slippery. If using fresh mushrooms, trim and wipe them.

2 Bring the dashi to a boil in an uncovered saucepan. Reduce the heat to low. Rub the miso through a sieve and stir it into the dashi, using a hand whisk. Add the radish and the mushrooms and simmer the soup for 5 to 6 minutes. Do not allow it to boil.

3 Meanwhile, wash the whole chives, if using, shake dry and cut into pieces about ¼ in. long.
4 Pour the soup into four soup bowls. Sprinkle with the chives, if using, and serve at once.

Note: The soup tastes equally good made with other types of mushrooms, such as ceps, chanterelles or slippery jacks. If using fresh mushrooms rather than canned ones, trim and wipe them before cooking.

Miso Soup

Quick • Basic recipe **Misoshiru** *Serves 4*

5.6 oz. fresh or vacuum-packed, firm tofu (see page 48)
2 thin leeks
10 pieces fresh ginger root
3 ½ cups dashi 2 (see page 28)
6 tbsp. miso (soybean paste see page 38), preferably equal proportions of white and red

Preparation time: 15 minutes (plus 30 minutes for preparing the dashi)

64 cal. per serving

1 Dip the tofu briefly in a bowl of cold water, drain, then cut into 1-in. dice.

2 Remove the wilted green leaves and roots of the leeks, then wash and cut into thin rings. Peel and finely grate the ginger to extract its juice.

3 Heat the dashi in an uncovered saucepan, but do not allow it to boil. Rub the miso through a sieve, then add it to the soup, stirring constantly with a hand-whisk, to prevent any lumps forming. Do not allow the soup to return to a boil.
4 Add the tofu, two thirds of the leek rings, and the ginger juice, and simmer for about 1 minute. Pour into small

individual bowls and serve garnished with the rest of the leek rings.

Variation: Miso soup with beef
Cut 7 oz. fillet steak into slices about ⅛ in. thick, and then into strips about 1 in. wide. Cut 2 oz. salsify (oyster plant) first into slices about ⅛ in. thick, and then into thin matchsticks. Cut ½ cup into ½ in. dice and 1 leek into rings about ¼ in. wide. Bring 3 ½ cups dashi 2 (see page 28) to a boil. Add the meat and salsify, bring briefly to a boil, then add the tofu and leeks and return to a boil. Rub 6 tbsp. miso through a sieve and stir into the soup. Bring briefly to a boil, then serve.

Mussels in Miso Soup

Takes time • Entrée   Asari no misoshiru   **Serves 4**

⅔ **cup mussels in their shells**
1 thin leek
1 ¼ cups dashi 2 (see page 28)
4 tbsp. white miso (see below)

**Preparation time: 45 minutes
(plus 30 minutes for preparing the
dashi)**

71 cal. per serving

1 In cold water, scrape, wash, and beard the mussels. Tap sharply any that are open, and discard those that don't close.

2 Cook the mussels in boiling water over medium heat for about 5 minutes, until the shells open. Remove them from the water, discarding any that are still closed. Strain the cooking water through cheesecloth, reserving 1 ¾ cups of it.

3 Remove the wilted green leaves and roots of the leeks, then wash the leeks

and cut them into thin rings. Bring the dashi and mussel water to a boil in an uncovered saucepan.

4 When the liquid begins to boil, rub the miso through a sieve, then add it to the soup, stirring constantly with a hand whisk to prevent any lumps forming. Remove the pan from the heat as soon as it returns to a boil.

5 Pour the soup into four individual soup bowls. Add the mussels and leek rings, and serve at once.

Miso

This highly nutritious, soft bean paste, with its pungent, salty flavor, is made by fermenting soybeans with rice or other grains. There are many different types of miso, and every region has its own version.
Miso falls into three categories. *Mamemiso* is made purely from soybeans, *mugimiso is* a blend of soybeans and barley, and *komemiso* – by far the most commonly used – is made from soybeans and rice.
The flavor and color, always shades of brown, varies, depending on the blend, but there are two basic types. *Shiromiso* (white miso) is an orange-brown color and tastes slightly sweet, while *akamiso* (red miso) is reddish-brown and tastes saltier. (The terms "white" and "red" used in the recipes

here are merely translations of the Japanese names.)
Miso is used frequently in Japanese cuisine. It is added to clear broth to make the thicker miso soup, which is eaten at breakfast time, but also very popular at lunch and dinner. It is also used in salad dressings and in the preparation of vegetable, fish, and other dishes. It also makes good flavoring for

casseroles and sauces; as it is very salty, there is usually no need to add further seasoning. Miso should be added toward the end of the cooking time, to prevent it from becoming lumpy. Miso is sold in packages in health food and specialty stores. It will keep for several months in the refrigerator. You can decant it into a glass jar, if preferred.

Salmon and Tofu Soup

Sake to tofu no shiru

1 x 7-oz. salmon steak,
filleted and skinned
salt
3 oz. daikon (Japanese white radish)
1 medium carrot
½ cup fresh, or vacuum-packed, firm
tofu (see page 48)
½ cup fresh leaf spinach
3 ½ cups Dashi 2 (see page 28)
2 tbsp. Japanese soy sauce

Preparation time: 45 minutes
(plus 1 hour's standing time and 30
minutes for making the dashi)

160 cal. per serving

1 Sprinkle both sides of the salmon with salt. Cover it and leave to stand in the refrigerator for about 1 hour. Peel the daikon, cut it lengthwise into four, and then into slices about ⅛ in. thick

2 Peel the carrots, cut them in half lengthwise and then into slices about ⅛ in. thick. Briefly dip the tofu in cold water, then drain and cut into eight equal-sized pieces.

3 Trim the spinach and then wash it thoroughly. Bring some water to a boil in a saucepan and blanch the spinach for about 1 minute. Remove from the water with a slotted spoon, and reserve.

4 Rinse the salmon, pat dry, and cut into 1 ½ in. dice. Bring the dashi to a boil in an uncovered saucepan. Add the daikon and carrots, and cook for about 5 minutes over medium heat.

5 Add the salmon and simmer in the hot soup for about 3 minutes. Add the tofu, spinach, and soy sauce, and return to a boil.

6 Pour the soup into four individual soup bowls and serve with rice.

Note: If you prefer a stronger flavor, season with a little more soy sauce.

Tofu Soup with Chicken

Easy • Entrée   **Kenchinjiru**   *Serves 4*

1 cup fresh, or vacuum-packed, firm
tofu (see page 48)
3 ½ oz. boned chicken thighs, with
skin
3 ½ oz. carrots
3 ½ oz. salsify (oyster plant)
3 ½ oz. daikon (Japanese white
radish)
2 oz. leek
4 in. square piece kombu seaweed
(see page 31)
1 tbsp. vegetable oil
2 tbsp. Japanese soy sauce

Preparation time: 45 minutes

100 cal. per serving

1 Briefly dip the tofu in cold water, drain and cut into ½ in. dice. Cut the chicken into 1 in. dice.

2 Peel the carrots, cut them in half lengthwise, and then into slices about ⅛ in. thick. Peel the salsify and cut into ⅛ in. slices.

3 Peel the daikon, cut it lengthwise into four pieces and then into slices about ⅛ in. thick.

4 Wash the leek and cut into rings about ¼ in. wide. Put 3 ½ cups water and the seaweed in a saucepan, and bring to a boil, removing the seaweed just before the water reaches boiling point. Reserve the water.

5 Heat the oil in a saucepan. Stir-fry the chicken and vegetables over high heat for about 3 minutes. Add the seaweed cooking water and simmer over medium heat for about 10 minutes. Skim off any fat globules with a spoon.

6 Add the diced tofu and simmer over low heat for about 2 minutes, then season with soy sauce.

7 Pour the soup into four individual soup bowls and serve at once.

Note: Kenchinjiru served with rice is a very popular lunch dish.

Drink: Japanese green tea is the classic accompaniment to this soup.

Belly of Pork in Dashi

Easy • Entrée **Tonjiru** *Serves 4*

7 oz. waxy potatoes
2 oz. carrots
5 ½ oz. onions
2 garlic cloves
4 x1-in. piece fresh ginger root
1 tbsp. vegetable oil
7 x 1/8 in. slices belly of pork (about 7 oz.)
3 ½ cups dashi 2 (see page 28)

Preparation time: 45 minutes (plus 30 minutes for making the dashi)

360 cal. per serving

1 Peel the potatoes and the carrots. Slice the carrots crosswise into 1-in. pieces, then cut the pieces in half lengthwise, and finally into matchsticks ½ in. wide. Cut the potatoes in half lengthwise, then cut the halves into matchsticks.

2 Peel the onions and cut them into thin rings. Peel and crush the garlic. Peel and finely grate the ginger.

3 Heat the oil in a flameproof casserole or saucepan and brown the ginger and garlic over high meat. Add the pork and the vegetables, and fry briefly.

4 Pour the dashi into the casserole or pan and simmer, uncovered, over low heat for 20 to 30 minutes. Skim the fat from the surface with a spoon.

5 Rub the miso through a sieve, then add it to the soup, stirring constantly with a hand whisk, to prevent any lumps forming. Bring very briefly to a boil, then pour into individual soup bowls, and serve.

Udon Noodle Soup

Takes time • Entrée **Tanuki udon** *Serves 4 to 6*

1 egg
7 tbsp. all-purpose flour
1 ¾ cupsl vegetable oil
½ cup fresh leaf spinach
4 pieces surimi (crabsticks)
1 baby leek
1 ½ oz. udon noodles
1 quart dashi 2 (see page 28)
⅔ cup Japanese soy sauce
2 tbsp. mirin (sweet rice wine)
2 tsp. sugar
seven-spice mixture (shichimio togarashi)

Preparation time: 1 hour (plus 30 minutes for preparing the dashi)

830 cal. per serving (if serving 6)

1 In a bowl, whisk the egg with 7 tbsp. water. Carefully stir in the flour, using the whisk to mix it in.

2 Heat the oil in a saucepan, until bubbles rise when you dip a wooden chopstick in it. Pour some over the egg and flour batter through a colander which has holes at least to ¼ in. in diameter, letting the drops of batter slide into the hot oil.

3 Fry the batter in batches for about 1 minute. Take care, as it may spit! Remove the fried batter from the pan with a slotted spoon, drain it, and set aside.

4 Trim and thoroughly wash the leaf spinach. Bring some water to a boil in a saucepan and blanch the spinach for about 3 minutes, drain it well and keep warm while cooking the noodles.

5 Cut the fish diagonally across the middle into strips. Remove the blanched green leaves and roots from the leek, then wash the leek thoroughly and cut into ¼ in. rings.

6 Bring plenty of water to a boil in a saucepan and boil the noodles for about 10 minutes, then drain.

7 Meanwhile, bring the dashi to a boil in a saucepan. In another pan, bring the soy sauce, mirin, and sugar briefly to a boil over high heat until the sugar has dissolved. Stir the soy sauce and mirin mixture into the dashi and remove from the heat.

8 Serve the noodles in four large soup bowls. Sprinkle the fried batter, fish, leek, and spinach on top and pour in the broth. Season the soup to taste with seven-spice mixture.

Noodles with Tempura

Takes time • Entrée **Tempura soba** *Serves 4*

2/3 cup mirin
(sweet rice wine)
6 cups dashi 2 (see page 28)
7 tbsp. Japanese soy sauce
2 thin leeks
1 sheet nori seaweed (see page 31)
8 raw shrimp, heads removed, each
weighing about 1 ounce
4 tbsp. all-purpose flour
plus extra for sprinkling
1 egg, straight from the refrigerator
7 tbsp. icewater
2 ¾ cups vegetable oil for frying
1 lb. soba noodles

Preparation time: 40 minutes
(plus 30 minutes for making the
dashi)

860 cal. per serving

1 Pour the mirin into a saucepan and boil briefly to evaporate the alcohol. Add the dashi and bring the mixture to a boil. Skim the scum from the top and stir in the soy sauce. Keep warm.

2 Remove the wilted green leaves and roots from the leeks, wash thoroughly and cut into ¼ in. rings. Briefly toast the seaweed on the electric hot plate or in a skillet without fat if cooking on gas, then cut into thin strips.

3 To shell the shrimp, split the shell on the underside with your thumb and remove the dark, vein-like intestine (*above*). Make small incisions about ½ in. apart along the underside of the shrimp so that they can be straightened easily.

4 To make the batter, sift the 4 tbsp. flour. Whisk the egg and the icewater together, then slowly stir in the flour, using a hand whisk to disperse any lumps.

5 Heat the oil until bubbles rise from a wooden chopstick dipped in the hot oil. If you are using an electric deep-fryer, preheat to 350° F.

6 Sprinkle the shrimp lightly with the remaining flour, coat them in batter, and

fry for about 1 minute, or until crisp. Take care as the oil may spit! Remove the shrimp from the pan with a slotted spoon, and drain on paper towels.

7 Bring a saucepan of water to a boil and add the noodles. Stir, then cook for about 5 minutes, until soft. If foam builds up in the pan, add more water. Drain, and rinse in cold water.

8 Divide the noodles between four individual soup bowls, and pour in the soup. Place two shrimp on top of each portion and sprinkle the seaweed and leek over them.

Note: Tempura consists of vegetables, shrimp, and fish dipped in thin batter and deep-fried in fresh vegetable oil. The ingredients for making the batter should be as cold as possible. This dish originated with the Portuguese missionaries who came to Japan in the 16th century.

Variation: Deep-fried fish and vegetables

To make tempura on its own, you need 8 shrimp, 1 oz. white fish, 1 oz. squid, 1 small eggplant, and 4 fresh shiitake mushrooms. Cut the fish and squid into four pieces. Wash and thinly slice the vegetables. Coat all the ingredients in bread crumbs and deep-fry as in the recipe above. Serve the vegetables and fish separately with a dip made from 1 cup Dashi 1, 4 tbsp. each of mirin and soy sauce, and side dishes of grated radish and ginger.

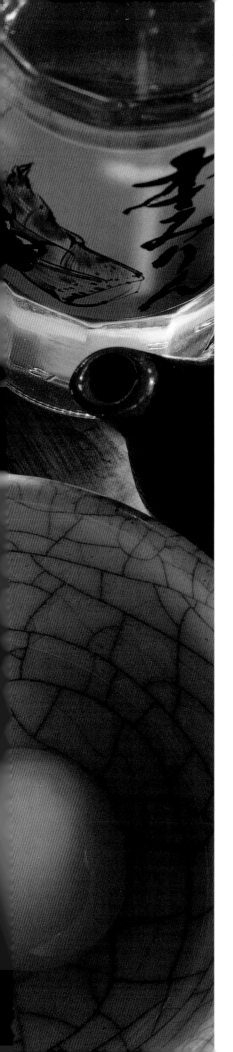

TOFU AND EGGS

T ofu, a soft, white, custard-like cake of soybean curd, is one of Japan's most important foods, and is eaten practically every day. Rich in vegetable protein and calcium, it features in a wide range of delicious and creative dishes that belie its bland appearance.

Tofu is an extremely versatile food: it can be fried, boiled, or broiled. In summer, it is often served cold, with grated ginger, green onions (scallions), and a soy sauce dip, accompanied by cold sake or beer. As a winter dish, it is heated through in seaweed-flavored water and served with a warmed dashi-soy sauce. Diced tofu is frequently added to soups, and is an essential ingredient in the famous beef fondue, sukiyaki.

This chapter includes a selection of classic dishes in which tofu is the main ingredient. However, it is also used in recipes featured elsewhere in the book. Recipes indicate whether the dish is intended as a side dish or entrée.

Eggs, while not a highly important element in Japanese cuisine, are becoming increasingly popular and are accorded the same flair and creativity in preparation as other foods. Among the best-loved dishes are delicate egg custards and omelets. *Chawanmushi*, a variety of ingredients such as chicken, shrimp, and mushrooms, gently steamed in an egg custard has become a classic. This dish, like tofu, can be eaten warm or cold, according to the time of year.

Fried Tofu

Easy • Entrée   **Tofu no usuage shogajoyu**   *Serves 4*

1 cup fresh, or vacuum-packed, firm tofu (see below)
7 tbsp. all-purpose flour
2 tbsp. vegetable oil
100 g daikon (Japanese white radish)
4 x1-in. piece fresh ginger root

For serving:
Japanese soy sauce

Preparation time: 20 minutes

170 cal. per serving

1 Dip the tofu briefly in cold water, drain and thoroughly pat dry. Carefully cut into eight equal-sized dice and coat in the flour.

2 Heat the oil in a skillet and fry the coated tofu over medium heat for about 1 minute on each side, until golden-brown.

3 Peel the radish and ginger, then finely grate them separately. Squeeze the juice from the daikon.

4 Arrange two pieces of tofu on each plate. Divide the grated daikon between the four plates, arranging it in a pile beside the tofu. Garnish with the grated ginger. Serve with a small bowl of soy sauce. A little soy sauce should be poured over the tofu before eating.

Note: You can also stir the ginger and radish into the soy sauce, then dip the tofu in the sauce before eating.

Variation: Deep-fried tofu

Cut 1 cup tofu into eight dice, coat in 7 tbsp. potato starch and deep-fry in 3 ½ cups oil. In a saucepan, mix 12 cups Dashi 2 (see page 28), 3 tbsp. soy sauce and 3 tbsp. mirin (see page 90), and bring briefly to a boil. Place two pieces of tofu in each soup bowl and pour the sauce over the top. Garnish with 6 tbsp. grated radish, 1 tbsp. grated ginger, and leek rings.

Tofu

Tofu is a white, custard-like cake of soybean curd, which ranges from firm to silken in consistency. It is an extremely nutritious food, being high in protein and low in fat, and is an essential ingredient in the cuisines of Japan and many other Far Eastern countries.

Invented in China over 2,000 years ago and introduced to Japan by early Buddhists, tofu was originally eaten only by monks in the temples. Today, it is enjoyed by everyone, and many family businesses make their living by supplying the population with the vast quantities it daily consumes.

Tofu is one of the most versatile of foods. Though it has very little flavor of its own, its texture combines well with all sorts of ingredients. It can be diced and fried, boiled, coated in bread crumbs, or puréed; it is eaten cold in the summer and warm in winter.

Fresh tofu is available in Japanese stores and large supermarkets. It will keep for two or three days if refrigerated in fresh cold water. It is also available canned and powdered.

Tofu Pancakes

Easy • Entrée **Tofu-iri o-konomiyaki** *Serves 4*

4 eggs
½ cup all-purpose flour
2 ¼ oz. peeled shrimp, heads and
intestines removed
2 ¼ oz. squid
2 ¼ oz. octopus
1 ⅓ lb. fresh, or vacuum-packed,
firm tofu (see page 48)
1 ¾ oz. fresh shiitake mushrooms
2 tbsp. Japanese soy sauce
2 tbsp. mirin (sweet rice wine)
1 tsp. potato starch
1 tbsp. vegetable oil
1 tbsp. hanakatsuo
(flaked, dried bonito)
1 tbsp. ao-nori
(flaked, dried green seaweed)
or chopped nori seaweed
(see page 31) for garnish

Preparation time: 50 minutes

330 cal. per serving

1 Whisk the eggs in a large bowl, then stir in the flour slowly with the whisk, to prevent lumps forming.

2 Wash and pat dry the shrimp, squid and octopus. Cut into ½ in. dice and add to the batter in the bowl.

3 Briefly dip the tofu in cold water, drain and thoroughly pat dry. Using a plastic spatula, crumble the tofu and fold it into the batter.

4 Wipe the mushrooms with a dry cloth, remove the stalks and cut the mushrooms into thin slices

5 Bring the soy sauce, mirin, and ½ cup water to a boil in a saucepan. Add the mushroom strips and simmer the mixture for about 10 minutes. Mix the potato starch with 1 tbsp. water and stir

it into the saucepan. Continue to stir until the sauce thickens.

6 Heat a little of the oil in a skillet about 6 inches in diameter, and pour in a quarter of the batter. Cook the pancake for about 2 minutes on each side, then place on a plate and keep warm while cooking three more pancakes.

7 Serve the pancakes in four separate shallow bowls. Pour the mushroom sauce over them and garnish with the hanakatsuo and seaweed.

Drinks: Sake, served warm or cold, goes well with the dish.

Chicken in Egg Custard

Chawanmushi

Prepare in advance • Appetizer

Serves 4

*2 oz. skinned chicken breast
fillet*
*4 raw jumbo shrimp (about
1 ½ oz. each)*
4 fresh shiitake mushrooms
salt
2 tbsp. sake (Japanese rice wine)
4 canned ginkgo nuts
2 eggs
*1 ¾ cups cooled dashi 2
(see page 28)*
2 tsp. Japanese soy sauce
2 tsp. mirin (sweet rice wine)
*mitsuba (Japanese parsley) or
Japanese cress for garnish*

*Preparation time: 35 minutes
(plus 30 minutes for preparing the
dashi)*

160 cal. per serving

1 Cut the chicken into four pieces. Wash and shell the shrimp, leaving the tails on, and removing the dark vein-like intestine (see Step 3, page 44). Wipe the mushrooms with a dry cloth and remove the stalks.

2 Season the chicken pieces, shrimp, and shiitake mushrooms with salt and sprinkle with sake. Drain the nuts.

3 Lightly whisk the eggs, but do not beat them to a froth. Add the dashi, soy sauce, and mirin. Strain the mixture through a sieve.

4 Arrange the chicken, shrimp, nuts, and mushrooms in four deep heatproof bowls or cups, and pour the egg mixture over them. Pour water into a large saucepan to a level of 1 inch. Cover the bowls with lids or plastic wrap, and place them in the water.

5 Heat the water until it begins to boil, then cover and steam the custards over low heat for about 15 to 20 minutes. To ensure that no condensation drips onto the custards, wrap the lid of the pan in a clean cloth. Do not allow the water in the pan to boil, or holes will form in the custards as they cook.

6 Garnish the custards with mitsuba or cress before serving.

Note: It is essential to provide spoons for this dish. Even the Japanese cannot manage chawanmushi with chopsticks!

Flaky Rolled Omelet

Dashimaki-tamago

More complicated • Entrée   *Serves 4*

1 fresh red chili pepper
(see Glossary)
7 tbsp. rice vinegar
6 tbsp. mirin (sweet rice wine)
5½ oz. daikon
(Japanese white radish)
salt
¾ cup cold dashi 1 (see page 28)
1 tsp. Japanese soy sauce
8 eggs
2 to 3 tbsp. vegetable oil

For serving:
Japanese soy sauce

Preparation time: 50 minutes
(plus 1 hour's marinating time and
15 minutes for making the dashi)

430 cal. per serving

1 Remove the stalk and seeds from the chili pepper. Wash and cut into thin rings. In a saucepan, bring the vinegar, 2 tbsp. of the mirin and 7 tbsp. water to a boil, then leave to cool.

2 Peel and very thinly slice the daikon. Sprinkle the slices with salt and knead thoroughly with your hands (see Note). Carefully rinse under cold running water to remove the salt, then squeeze the daikon thoroughly. Place in a bowl, pour the vinegar mixture over it, and leave to marinate, uncovered, for about 1 hour at room temperature.

3 Mix the dashi with the soy sauce and the remaining mirin. Whisk the eggs in a bowl, the carefully stir them into the dashi and mirin mixture.

4 Heat a little oil in a large skillet (a rectangular one, if possible). Spread a ladleful of batter thinly over the bottom of the pan, and fry over steady medium heat for about 15 seconds. If any bubbles form, press them flat.

5 When the batter is nearly cooked, i.e. the surface is not very quite set and the batter is still bubbling round the edges, gradually roll the omelet to the far end of the pan, then grease the pan again and add another ladleful of batter, lifting the finished

omelet slightly so that the batter runs underneath (*below left*).

6 Fry the batter as before and then roll it around the first omelet (*above*). Repeat eight times, each time adding a further layer to the rolled omelet.

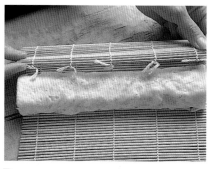

7 Wrap the rolled omelet in a makisu (bamboo mat used for rolling sushi) or a clean cloth (*above*), so that it keeps its shape. leave it to stand for about 10 minutes, then carefully remove the bamboo mat or cloth.

8 Cut the roll into ¾ inch-wide strips and serve. Sprinkle the daikon with chili pepper rings and serve as a side dish, and the soy sauce as a dip.

Note: Kneading vegetables until they are soft is a widely used technique in Japan. Vegetables such as eggplant, daikon, carrots, and cabbage tenderized in this way do not need to be cooked.

Egg Sushi with Shrimp

More complicated • Main course **Ebi kimizushi** *Serves 4 (8 pieces)*

8 raw jumbo shrimp, each weighing
about 1 ½ oz (heads removed)
salt
2 eggs
6 egg yolks
3 tsp. sugar
8 tsp. rice vinegar
Japanese cress for garnish
(optional)

For serving:
Japanese soy sauce

Preparation time: 30 minutes

260 cal. per piece

1 Make shallow incisions about 1 in. apart along the underside of the shrimp and thread each one lengthwise onto a skewer so that it is straight.

2 Cook the shrimp, covered, in salted water over medium heat for about 5 minutes. leave to cool, then pull the shrimp off the skewers. Shell them and remove the dark vein-like intestine (see Step 3, page 44).

3 Heat the eggs, egg yolks, sugar, and a pin. of salt in a heatproof bowl placed over a saucepan of gently simmering water, stirring constantly. When the mixture begins to set, add the vinegar.

Continue to stir until it sets again, then pass the mixture through a sieve.

4 Moisten the palms of your hands and shape the mixture into eight cylinders, like sushi rolls. Place a shrimp on top of each one, then arrange some cress beside the egg sushi as a garnish, if wished. Serve the soy sauce as a dip.

Note: When dipping these sushi, make sure that you dip only the shrimp side into the soy sauce, since the egg easily falls apart if it comes into contact with the liquid. Egg sushi is also delicious made with salmon instead of shrimp.

Egg Rolls

Simple • Appetizer **Datemaki-tamago** *Serves 4*

5½ oz. raw jumbo shrimp
1 ½ tsp. salt
8 eggs
1 ½ tbsp. sugar
10 tbsp. sake (Japanese rice wine)
1 tbsp. vegetable oil

For serving:
Japanese soy sauce

Preparation time: 1 hour

430 cal. per serving

1 Wash and shell shrimp, leaving the tails on. Remove the dark vein-like intestines (see Step 3, page 44). Pat the shrimp dry and chop finely. Using a pestle and mortar, grind the shrimp to a paste with the salt.

2 Separate the eggs. Slowly stir the egg whites into the shrimp paste, one at a time. Then stir in the sugar, sake, and finally the egg yolks.

3 Heat the oil in a large skillet (a rectangular one, if possible). Pour in the egg batter and fry over low heat for 15 to 20 minutes. When the edges turn golden, turn the omelet and fry on the other side until golden. Carefully burst any air bubbles with a fork.

4 Turn off the heat. Place a lid directly onto the omelet to weigh it down. leave it to stand for about 10 minutes, so that no more air bubbles form.

5 Roll the omelet, Swiss-roll style, with a makisu (bamboo mat used for rolling sushi) or a clean cloth. Leave to stand briefly, then carefully remove the mat or cloth. Cut the egg roll with a sharp knife into slices about 1 in. wide. Serve with soy sauce as a dip.

Note: It is nice to include egg rolls if you are making a dish of different sushi (see pages 110 and 114).

Layered Egg Cake

Nishoku-tamago

More complicated • Appetizer

Serves 4 (8 slices)

12 eggs
salt
vinegar
4 tbsp. sugar
8 chives

For serving:
Japanese soy sauce

Preparation time: 55 minutes

570 cal. per slice

1 Hard-boil the eggs in water with salt and vinegar added. Rinse them in cold water, then leave to cool.

2 Shell the eggs and separate the yolks and whites (*above*). Press separately through a sieve into two bowls, and stir 2 tbsp. sugar and ½ tsp. salt into each.

3 Spread the egg whites in a layer in a 8-in. square dish or a 9-in. long terrine dish and press gently. Spread the egg yolks over them (*above*) and smooth the top, pressing down gently.

4 Fill a large saucepan (large enough to stand the dish in) about one third full of water and bring to a boil over high heat. Place the dish in the bain-marie. Wrap a clean cloth around the lid of the pan to avoid condensation dripping onto the eggs. Cover the pan and cook the eggs in the bain-marie over medium heat for 4 to 5 minutes.

5 Leave the egg cake to cool, then cut into eight equal-sized slices. Serve two slices on each plate, with the yolk side upward. Garnish each portion with two chives and serve the Japanese soy sauce as a dip.

Drink: Sake is the perfect drink to serve with this dish.

Note: In Japan, a special aluminum dish 8 in. square and about 1¾ inches deep, called a *nagashikan*, is used for making layered egg cake. It has a special aluminum attachment for lifting the cake out of the dish.

Variation: Prepare the layered egg cake as described. Tear 2 pieces of *surimi* (crabsticks) into small pieces and press gently into the cooled cake. Place a saucepan lid on top to weigh it down. Press the cake for about 1 hour before serving.

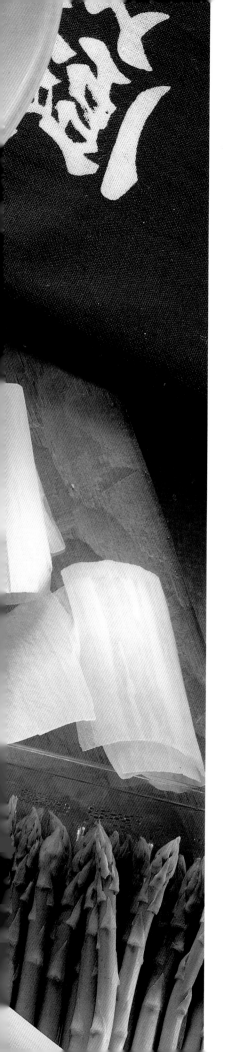

SALADS AND VEGETABLES

T hanks to specialty farming methods, Japan today enjoys a rich variety of fresh fruit and vegetables, available year round. For the majority of Japanese, however, the primary consideration in choosing vegetables is still whether or not they are in season, for it is firmly believed that a food is inseparable from its season. Freshness is another priority for the Japanese cook, who will often choose her vegetables according to what looks best in the market that day, and then decide how to cook them.

Vegetables are prepared in a variety of ways, the favorite methods being boiling, steaming, and pickling. They are always cooked gently, so that they remain crisp; and to ensure that they retain their natural flavor, relatively few seasonings are used, just soy sauce, mirin, dashi, and sake. Ginger is sometimes added, too, to give fresh tangy flavor. Salads in Japan, unlike their Western equivalents which are usually made with raw ingredients, are often composed of cooked vegetables served with soy sauce or vegetables pickled in vinegar.

Small portions of different vegetables or salads can be served as a appetizer, a side dish, or an entrée. The recipes in this chapter indicate how each dish is intended to be served.

Although many of the vegetables eaten in Japan are available in the United States, they tend to differ in size, so it is often best to buy them from stores specializing in oriental foods.

Pear with Sesame Seeds

Yonashi to kyuri no gama-ae

2 tbsp. white sesame seeds
1 tbsp. Japanese soy sauce
½ tbsp. sugar
1 pear
salt
1 small cucumber

Preparation time: 30 minutes

60 cal. per serving

1 Heat a nonstick skillet without oil until very hot, then toast the sesame seeds over medium heat for 3 minutes, or until golden. Shake the pan back and forth over the heat, so that the sesame seeds do not burn.

2 Coarsely crush the sesame seeds, using a pestle and mortar or suribachi, a special ribbed bowl used in Japan for grinding ingredients (*above*). Stir in the soy sauce and sugar.

3 Peel the pear, cut in half lengthwise, and remove the core. Cut lengthwise into eighths and then into slices about ⅛ in. thick. Trim the edges to make rounded shapes, then soak the slices in cold salted water for about 3 minutes.

4 Thoroughly wash the cucumber, cut it in half lengthwise and scrape out all the seeds with a teaspoon. Cut the two lengths crosswise onto slices about ⅛ in. thick. Place in a bowl, sprinkle with salt and leave to stand for about 10 minutes, to draw out the juices, then gently squeeze out the liquid.

5 Remove the pear from the water and pat dry. Add the slices to the cucumber, stir in the sesame seed dressing, and serve on individual plates.

Note: You can buy ready-toasted sesame seeds. However, if you toast your own, the dish acquires a more pungent sesame flavor. Sesame seeds can also be sprinkled on breads, cakes, and cookies before they are baked. Black sesame seeds are also used, though less common than white. They taste the same as the white but add dramatic color to baked foods.

Variation: Sesame seed dressing is equally delicious served with green beans. Trim and wash ¾ cup fresh green beans, and cook them in salted water for about 5 minutes. Drain and rinse in cold water. Chop the beans into ⅛ in. pieces. Prepare the sesame dressing as in step 2, adding 1 tsp. Dashi 1 (see page 28), if wished. Mix with the beans and serve.

Stuffed Shiitake Mushrooms

Ebi to shiitake no futamiage

More complicated • Appetizer

Serves 4

5 ½ oz. raw shelled jumbo shrimp, deveined, heads removed (see Step 3, page 44)
3 tbsp. mayonnaise
8 fresh shiitake mushrooms, about 2 inches in diameter
4 green asparagus spears
6 tbsp. all-purpose flour plus extra for coating
7 tbsp. ice water
1 egg yolk
1 quart vegetable oil for deep-frying
For serving:
Japanese soy sauce

Preparation time: 45 minutes (plus 1 hour's chilling time)

520 cal. per serving

1 Finely chop the shrimp and crush them, using a pestle and mortar. Mix with the mayonnaise, cover, and chill in the refrigerator for about 1 hour.

2 Using a dry cloth, carefully wipe the grit from the mushrooms, and discard the stalks (*above*). Peel and trim the asparagus spears, and cut into 2 inches pieces.

3 Sift the 3 tbsp. flour. Mix the cold water and egg yolk in a bowl, then lightly stir in the flour. It does not matter if some of the flour is still visible.

4 Sprinkle the underside of each of the mushroom caps with flour, tapping to remove any surplus. Spoon the shrimp mixture into the mushroom caps, filling them generously so that the stuffing is heaped in the mushrooms (*above*).

5 Coat the shrimp-stuffed mushrooms in flour, tapping to remove any surplus. Coat the asparagus lengths in flour, then dip the mushrooms and asparagus in the batter.

6 Heat the oil in a deep skillet or deep-fat fryer, until bubbles rise when you dip a wooden chopstick in it. If you are using an electric deep-fryer, heat the oil to 350 degrees. Deep-fry the stuffed mushrooms and asparagus for about 2 minutes.

7 Arrange the cooked mushrooms and asparagus on four serving plates. Serve the vegetables accompanied by the soy sauce in a separate bowl as a dip.

Note: After cooking, drain the cold or lukewarm oil through a sieve lined with paper towels. The oil can then be used another three or four times for deep-frying vegetables.

Vegetable Stew

Gomoku-ni

Takes time • Entrée

Serves 4

⅓ cup dried soybeans
8 dried shiitake mushrooms
1 tbsp. rice vinegar (su)
2 medium-sized waxy potatoes
1 medium-sized carrot
¾ cup canned bamboo shoots
7 tbsp. sugar snap peas
salt
¾ cup Dashi 2 (see page 28)
2 heaping tbsp. sugar
1 tbsp. mirin (sweet rice wine)
2 tbsp. Japanese soy sauce
shiso leaves (see Glossary) or fresh
herbs for garnish (optional)

Preparation time: 1 hour
(plus 12 hours soaking time and
30 minutes for making the dashi)

230 cal. per serving

1 Soak the beans in 1 quart water for about 12 hours. Soak the lotus root and mushrooms in separate bowls of water for the same time, changing the water from time to time.

2 Remove any beans that have floated to the surface, then drain off the water. Bring a saucepan of water to a boil and boil the beans for 10 minutes, then simmer, uncovered, over medium heat for about 1 hour, until tender.

3 Drain the lotus root and mushrooms. Cut the mushrooms into four, discarding the stalks. Cook the lotus root, uncovered, in a saucepan of water with the
rice vinegar added, over medium heat for 8 minutes. Drain, and reserve.

4 Wash and peel the potatoes, and cut them into walnut-sized pieces. Peel the carrot and cut it into 1 in. dice. Cook the

potatoes and carrot in a little water in an uncovered pan over medium heat for 8 to 10 minutes; drain and reserve.

5 Drain the bamboo shoots, cut them into walnut-sized pieces, and boil for about 15 minutes. Trim the sugar peas, cut them ¾ inch-long pieces and cook for about 1 minute in salted water (so that they stay green.) Drain and reserve.

6 Place all the prepared ingredients except the peas, in a large pan with the dashi, sugar, and mirin. Place a small saucepan lid on top of the vegetables to weigh them down and ensure that they cook evenly. Simmer over low heat for about 15 minutes.

7 Add the soy sauce and simmer for a further 15 minutes. Stir in the sugar snap peas, and simmer for 1 minute. Serve the stew warm or cold, garnished with shiso leaves (see Glossary) or fresh herbs, if wished.

Sesame Spinach

Simple • Appetizer

Horenso no gomayogoshi

Serves 4

1 ½ cups fresh leaf spinach
salt
1 tbsp. tahini (white sesame paste)
2 tsp. white miso
(soybean paste see page 38)
4 tsp. Japanese soy sauce
4 tsp. sugar
2 tsp. mirin (sweet rice wine)
fresh herbs for garnish (optional)

Preparation time: 30 minutes

79 cal. per serving

1 Trim the spinach, removing the stalks. Cut large leaves in half, then wash thoroughly. Bring a little salted water to a boil in a saucepan and blanch the spinach for 1 to 2 minutes.

2 Remove the spinach from the water, using a slotted spoon, and drain in a colander. Lay the spinach briefly in ice-cold water to cool it, then drain it in the colander again.

3 In a bowl, mix together the tahini, miso, soy sauce, sugar, and mirin. Stir in the spinach.

4 Transfer the salad to small individual bowls to serve, and garnish with fresh herbs, if wished.

Note: Do not use frozen spinach for this recipe.

Variation: Spinach salad
Trim and thoroughly wash 1 ½ cups fresh leaf spinach and blanch for 2 minutes. Pour off the water, drain thoroughly, and then cut into 1 ½ in. pieces. Make a dressing by mixing 1 ½ tbsp. soy sauce and 3 tbsp. dashi 1 (see page 28). Stir one third of the soy dressing into the spinach. Serve in four small individual bowls, and pour over the rest of the dressing. Garnish with hanakatsuo (flaked, dried bonito) – about 1 tbsp. per serving.

Cabbage and Steak Salad

Gyushabu salad *Serves 4*

For the pon-zu dressing:
¾ cup yuzu juice or lemon juice
10 tbsp. rice vinegar (su)
¾ cup Japanese soy sauce
4 tbsp. mirin (sweet rice wine)
1 heaping tbsp. hanakatsuo
(flaked, dried bonito)
2-in. square sheet kombu seaweed
(see page 31)
Other ingredients:
7 oz. fillet steak (ask your
butcher to cut into strips about
⅛ nch thick)
10½ oz. Chinese (Napa)
cabbage or 1 small iceberg lettuce
3½ oz. leeks
14 oz. daikon (Japanese white
radish)
3½ oz. carrots
1 dried red chili pepper (see
Glossary
finely chopped chives for garnish
(optional)

Preparation time: 45 minutes
(plus 2 days for pickling the
dressing)

190 cal. per serving

1 To make the pon-zu dressing, mix the yuzu juice, rice vinegar, soy sauce, mirin, hanakatsuo and seaweed in a jar. Cover and leave to stand in the refrigerator for 2 days. Strain the dressing through a cloth or filter bag into a small serving bowl. Set aside.

2 Bring a saucepan of water to a boil and blanch the steak strips for about 3 minutes (*above*). Transfer the steak to a bowl of ice-cold water and leave to cool briefly. Remove it from the water and drain in a colander.

3 Trim and wash the Chinese (Napa) cabbage and cut it crosswise into pieces.

4 Trim the wilted leaves and roots from the leeks. Wash the leeks and slice thinly, using a cucumber slicer.

5 Peel the daikon and carrots. Cut off and reserve a piece of the daikon about 2 inches long. Very thinly slice the rest

of the daikon and carrots. (This is easily done with an asparagus peeler). Using a sharp knife, cut the thinly sliced daikon and carrots into very thin strips. (*below left*).

6 With the point of a knife, bore a small hole in the middle of the reserved piece of daikon. Remove the seeds from the chili pepper if wished, then put the chili in the hole in the daikon, and grate finely (*above*). The mixture should be pink and not too fiery. If necessary, remove the chili from the daikon when you think the flavor and color are strong enough.

7 Arrange the Chinese cabbage, leeks and strips of daikon and carrot on four individual plates. Place the meat on top and grated daikon and chili on the side. Sprinkle a few chopped chives over the meat to garnish, if wished. Serve with the pon-zu dressing.

Drink: Cold sake goes perfectly with this refreshing dish.

Salsify with Sesame Seeds

Kinpira-gobo

8 oz. salsify (oyster plant)

3 oz. carrots

1 tbsp. rice vinegar (su)

3 tbsp. vegetable oil

3 tbsp. sugar

3 tbsp. Japanese soy sauce

1 tbsp. white sesame seeds or
toasted sesame seeds

seven-spice mixture (see Note)

Preparation time: 50 minutes

130 cal. per serving

1 Peel the salsify and carrots, then cut them lengthwise into thin slices. Cut then slices into ⅛ in. pieces and then into thin strips. In a bowl, mix the rice vinegar with 1 quart water and soak the salsify for about 10 minutes.

2 Drain the salsify and pat dry. Heat the oil in a skillet or saucepan and fry the salsify and carrots over medium heat for about 5 minutes. Add the sugar and soy sauce and cook, uncovered, for a further 5 minutes or until all the liquid has evaporated.

3 Meanwhile, toast the sesame seeds in a skillet without oil over medium heat for about 3 minutes, shaking the skillet back and forth over the heat, so that the sesame seeds do not burn.

4 Add the toasted sesame seeds to the vegetables, season them to taste with the seven-spice mixture, and serve.

Variation:

Marinated Carrots and Radish

Peel 11 ½ oz. daikon (Japanese white radish). Cut crosswise into pieces about 2 inches long, then lengthwise into thin slices and finally into very thin strips. Peel 2 oz. carrots and cut in the same way as the daikon. Keeping the two vegetables separate, sprinkle with salt, then leave them to stand for about 10 minutes, until soft. Rinse thoroughly under running cold water to remove the salt, then squeeze dry by hand. In a bowl mix 1 tbsp. rice vinegar, ½ tsp. sugar and 1 tsp. dashi 1 (see page 28) to make a marinade, and marinate the vegetables for at least 12 hours.

Note: Seven-spice mixture (shichimi togarashi) is a peppery, chili-based spice mixture, good sprinkled over vegetables or grilled meat. It is available from specialty food stores.

Boiled Daikon

Furofuki daikon *Serves 4*

10 ½ oz. daikon (Japanese
white radish)
4 by 6 inches sheet kombu seaweed
(see page 31)
4 tsp. mirin (sweet rice wine)
½ cup white miso (soybean paste
see page 38)
2 tbsp. Dashi 1 (see page 28)
1 egg yolk

Preparation time: 30 minutes
(plus 30 minutes cooking time and
15 minutes for making the dashi)

150 cal. per serving

1 Carefully peel the daikon and cut into slices about 1 in. thick. Trim the edges with a knife to create rounded shapes. Boil the daikon in a saucepan of water over medium heat for about 10 minutes to remove the bitter taste. Drain and set aside.

2 Meanwhile, wipe the seaweed with a damp cloth, then soak it in a saucepan containing 6 cups water for about 20 minutes.

3 Add the daikon to the seaweed and bring the water to a boil, then discard the seaweed. Simmer the daikon, uncovered, over low heat for about 30 minutes, until tender.

4 Meanwhile, 5 minutes before the end of the daikon cooking time, place the mirin, miso, sugar, and dashi in another saucepan and heat through over low heat. Stir in the egg yolk and simmer for about 5 minutes, stirring constantly.

5 Drain the daikon and serve on four individual plates, with the sauce.

Drink: Sake goes well with this dish.

Note: Boiled daikon can be served warm as a entrée, if preferred. Other mild-flavored vegetables such as kohlrabi or white turnips can be prepared in the same way.

Eggplant with Chicken

Quick • Appetizer **Nasu torisoboro** *Serves 4*

1 eggplant
7 tbsp. vegetable oil
2 oz. leeks
3 tbsp. potato starch
3 ½ oz. boned chicken
¼ cup Dashi 2 (see page 28)
4 tbsp. mirin (sweet rice wine)
2 tsp. Japanese soy sauce

Preparation time: 30 minutes (plus 30 minutes for making the dashi)

330 calories per serving

1 Wash the eggplant, discard the stem, and cut the eggplant in half lengthwise. Using a knife or vegetable peeler, cut a decorative, criss-cross pattern in the skin (*above*).

2 Preheat the oven to 450 degrees. Cut the eggplant halves in half lengthwise again, and then cut into ¾ in. dice. Pierce the dice with a fork (*above*), and then soak in a bowl containing 6 tbsp. of the vegetable oil for about 1 minute.

3 Fry the diced eggplant in a skillet, without any additional oil, over medium heat for about 5 minutes, until browned on all sides.

4 Transfer the browned pieces to an ovenproof dish and bake in the center of the oven for about 5 minutes, or until the eggplant is soft.

5 Trim the wilted green leaves and roots from the leeks, then wash them thoroughly to remove any dirt and grit, and cut into thin rings. Set aside

6 In a bowl, mix the potato starch with 2 cups water, using a hand-whisk.

7 Grind the chicken in a food processor, then stir-fry in a skillet or saucepan with 1 tbsp. oil over high heat for about
2 minutes. Add the dashi to the pan and bring to a boil, uncovered. Skim off any bubbles of fat with a spoon.

8 Season the sauce with the mirin and soy sauce, then stir in the potato starch solution, using the hand whisk; return the mixture to a boil.

9 Divide the sauce between four individual plates. Arrange the cooked eggplant on top, with the skin side upward (so that pattern shows). Serve garnished with the leek rings.

Note: This eggplant dish can be served as an appetizer before a meal, or as an entrée. If you like, prepare double the quantity and serve half warm for dinner and the rest for lunch the following day, warm or cold.
The chicken sauce also goes well with boiled vegetables, such as daikon (Japanese white radish) – see recipe, page 69.

RICE

I t is hard to imagine a Japanese meal without rice, one of this island nation's most important foods. And not surprisingly, given its prominence in the daily diet, the Japanese are very particular about the quality of the rice they eat. Throughout the country there are specialty stores selling different grades of rice imported from a variety of growing areas.

If a meal consists of several courses, the rice is served as a side dish with the entrée, or separately at the end of the meal, accompanied by tea. The rice is then eaten on its own and not mixed with other foods. It is quite unusual to pour sauce over rice.

If rice is served as the entrée, the meal takes a different form. For the popular rice hotpots ingredients such as vegetables, fish, or meat are cooked with the rice. The celebrated Japanese tidbits known as sushi, made from vinegar-flavored rice and raw fish, are also served as a entrée. Since the sushi recipes in this book are mostly made with fish, they are included in the chapter beginning on page 99.

Ceremonial foods are a popular part of Japanese culture. On festive occasions, *sekihan* (red rice), a dish of red adzuki beans and rice, is served. Red being traditionally regarded as symbol of good luck, it is still the custom in some rural areas to offer this dish as a gift to friends and neighbors on the birth of a child, on the first day at school, or at wedding.

Rice Hotpot

Easy • Entrée   **Zosui**   *Serves 4*

1 cup cooked medium-grain
California rice
1 quart meat or vegetable broth
(can be made with a broth cube)
3 tbsp. Japanese soy sauce
4 egg yolks
½ sheet nori seaweed (see page 31),
cut into strips for garnish

Preparation time: 20 minutes

290 cal. per serving

1 Boil the cooked rice in the broth for 5 minutes, stirring from time to time and skimming off any scum from the surface. Cover and simmer over low heat for a further 5 minutes.

2 Add the soy sauce to the rice, then transfer the rice to deep individual bowls and place an egg yolk in the middle of each. Cut the seaweed into long thin strips with kitchen scissors. Sprinkle it over the rice and serve at once.

Drink: Traditional Japanese green tea goes best with this dish.

Note: This hotpot is known as zosui if the rice is cooked in meat or vegetable broth. If water or dashi is used to cook the rice, it is called kayu.
Make sure you use very fresh eggs from a reliable source of this recipe, to reduce any risk of salmonella.

Variation: This dish can be enhanced by adding vegetables, fish or meat. For example, trim and thinly slice about ½ cup vegetables per person (such as carrots, daikon, leeks) and cook with the rice.

Rice

Rice, regarded as a gift of the gods, is Japan's staple food. In ancient times, it was seen not only as a food, but also as an indication of wealth, and was used as currency. Today, the rice harvest is still a time for general celebration and thanksgiving.

Rice is enjoyed in many different ways. It is served daily at breakfast, lunch, and dinner, either with or just after the entrée. It is fermented to make into rice wines (sake and mirin), and it is also used to make rice vinegar (su).

There are two main categories of rice eaten in Japan, both of which are high in starch. They are round-grain rice, and sweet, glutinous rice, known as *mochi-gome*. Authentic Japanese round-grain rice is, unfortunately, not available outside Japan. Because

there is only limited space for its cultivation in Japan, the home-grown rice is kept exclusively for the domestic market. A good substitute is California medium-grain rice, which has plumper grains than long-grain, and absorbs more liquid while cooking. Glutinous rice (also sold as "sticky" or "sweet" rice) has cream-colored oval grains which cook to a sticky mass. In Japan, this type of rice

is used to make rice cakes and candies.

The amount of water required to cook rice varies according to the length of time it has been stored since it was harvested. The Japanese prepare rice in special cookers that work on the same principle as steamers. The rice is cooked with water but without salt.

Rice Triangles

Sanshoku o-nigiri

Can be made in advance • Entrée

Serves 4

3.5 oz. salmon fillet
salt
4 cups medium-grain California rice
5 umeboshi (Japanese pickled plums)
1 heaped tbsp. hanakatsuo (flaked, dried bonito)
2 sheets of nori seaweed (see page 31)
pickles for garnish (optional)
For serving:
Japanese soy sauce

Preparation time: 45 minutes (plus 1 hour for drying the salmon)

860 kJ/200cal. per triangle

1 Preheat the oven to 400° F.

2 Sprinkle the salmon with salt. To dry the salmon, place it on a rack, with a pan underneath to catch the juice, in the center of the oven for 1 hour. Then grind it, using a pestle and mortar or food processor.

3 Place the rice in a sieve and wash it three or four times until the water runs clear, then leave to drain. Place the rice in a saucepan with 3½ cups water. Bring to boil and cook over low heat for about 25 minutes. Place a folded kitchen towel between the saucepan and the lid, to absorb the steam.

4 Pit the umeboshi and mash them to a paste with a fork. Season one bowl with the hankatsuo, another with the dried salmon, and the third with the umeboshi paste.

5 Using kitchen scissors, cut the first sheet of seaweed lengthwise into three pieces, then cut them in half, to give six 2 by 4 in. strips (*above*).

6 Repeat the process with the second sheet to give a total of 12 strips of the seaweed.

7 Moisten your hands with water, then shape the rice in each of the bowls into four small balls. Squeeze them firmly, then shape into triangles (*above*).

8 Wrap each triangle in a strip of seaweed, so that the apex of the rice triangle is still visible (*above*).

9 Arrange the triangles on a serving dish. Garnish with pickles, such as pickled radish, if wished, and serve with the soy sauce as a dip.

Drink: Japanese green tea is the best accompaniment to this dish.

Note: The rice can be seasoned with other ingredients of your choice. Stores specializing in oriental foods sell a variety of ready-made rice seasonings. They also sell rice molds. These rice triangles can be made in advance and are great for picnics.

Rice with chicken

Takes time • Entrée **Soboro gohan**

1¼ cups medium-grain
California rice

7 oz. boned, skinned chicken legs
or chicken breast fillets

5 tbsp. sugar

2 tbsp. Japanese soy sauce

½ cup sugar snap peas

salt

3 eggs

5 tbsp. sake (Japanese rice wine)

Preparation time: 45 minutes

600 cal. per serving

1 Wash the rice in a bowl three or four times, or until the water runs clear, then drain through a sieve.

2 Place the washed rice in a saucepan with about 2 ½ cups water. Bring to a boil and cook over low heat for about 25 minutes. Place a folded kitchen towel between the saucepan and the lid, to absorb the steam.

3 Meanwhile, grind the chicken in a food processor.

4 Place the chicken in a saucepan with 2 tbsp. of the sugar and the soy sauce, and cook, uncovered, over high heat for about 15 minutes, until all the liquid has evaporated. Stir from time to time while the chicken is cooking. Remove the pan from the heat and set aside.

5 Trim and wash the sugar snap peas, and cut diagonally into 1-in. pieces. Bring some salted water to a boil in a saucepan and blanch the sugar snap peas for about 1 minute. Drain and rinse with cold water.

6 Mix the eggs with the remaining sugar, the sake, and salt to taste, and cook like scrambled eggs in a nonstick skillet, until crisp and dry.

7 Serve the rice in four soup bowls, followed by the ground chicken, and top with the fried egg. Garnish with sugar peas before serving.

Pot Rice with Steak

Takes time • Winter dish

Kamameshi

Serves 4

1¾ cups medium-grain California rice
⅓ cup thawed frozen peas
2½ cups Dashi 2 (see page 28)
1 tbsp. sugar
2 tbsp. Japanese soy sauce
6 tbsp. sake (Japanese rice wine)
11 oz. fillet steak, cut into thin strips

Preparation time: 1 hour
(plus 30 minutes for making the dashi)

520 cal. per serving

1 Wash the rice in a bowl three or four times, or until the water runs clear, then drain through a sieve.

2 Place the washed rice in a saucepan with about 2½ cups water, bring to a boil, and cook over medium heat for about 25 minutes. Place a folded kitchen towel between the saucepan and the lid, to absorb the steam.

3 Bring some water to a boil in a pan and blanch the peas for 30 seconds, then drain and rinse in cold water.

4 Bring ¾ cup of the dashi to a boil in a saucepan with the sugar, 1 tbsp. of the soy sauce, and 1 tsp. of the sake. Add the steak and cook over medium heat for about 1 minute. Add the peas and cook for another minute. Remove from the heat and leave to cool.

5 Divide the rice between four small, lidded pots. Divide the remaining dashi, sake, and soy sauce between the four portions and stir into the rice. Replace the pot lids.

6 Fill a large saucepan with water to a level of about 2 inches and place the small pots in the water. Bring to a boil and simmer the rice in the bain-marie over medium heat for about 15 minutes.

7 Lay a quarter of the cooked steak and a quarter of the peas on top of each portion of rice in the pots. Cover and steam over medium heat for a further 10 minutes, until the rice is cooked through evenly. Serve the rice and steak in the little pots.

Note: The steak and peas should be stirred into the rice before eating.

Red Festival Rice

More complex • Entrée   **Sekihan**   *Serves 4*

1 ¾ cups glutinous rice
⅓ cup dried adzuki beans
salt
black sesame seeds for garnish
(optional)

Preparation time: 1 hour
(plus 1 hour's cooking time)

600 cal. per serving

1 Wash the rice thoroughly and leave to stand in a bowl with 1 quart water for about 1 hour. Meanwhile, wash the adzuki beans, place them in a saucepan with 1 quart water and bring to a boil. Drain the beans as soon as the water starts to bubble.

2 Return the beans to a boil again with fresh water and cook, uncovered, over medium heat for 50 minutes, or until tender, checking from time to time that there is enough water in the pan and topping up with more, if necessary.

3 Drain the rice. Fill a large saucepan with water up to a level of about 2 inches. Suspend a steamer attachment or sieve over the pan, making sure that it does not come into contact with the water. Place a clean cloth over the steamer and spoon the rice into the cloth.

4 Bring the water to a boil, cover the rice, and steam over medium heat for about 20 minutes. If all water boils away, top up with a little more boiling water. Remove the pan from the heat and set aside.

5 Leave the cooked beans to cool in the saucepan for about 20 minutes. Lay a damp cloth over the steamer or sieve to prevent the beans drying out.

6 When the beans are cool, drain them through a sieve, reserving the cooking water. Bring ¾ cup of the bean water, ⅔ cup water, and a pin. of salt to a boil in a saucepan.

7 Add the rice to a boiling water and continue to cook until all the liquid is absorbed, stirring the rice with a ladle from time to time.

8 Carefully stir the adzuki beans into the rice and leave to stand in a warm place for about 20 minutes. Stir the mixture again before serving.

9 Serve the rice in four individual bowls and garnish with black sesame seeds, if liked.

Note: Sekihan is a typical festival dish. Served warm or cold, it is eaten on its own at the end of the meal.
Steaming, widely used in Japan, is a particularly gentle way of cooking that brings out all the characteristic flavors of ingredients.
If you prefer a spicier flavor, add 1 tsp. toasted sesame seeds and an extra pin. of salt to the cooked beans and rice.

MEAT AND POULTRY

For many years meat eating was forbidden in Japan, since Buddhism prohibited the the slaughter of animals. It was not until 1873 that the ban was lifted by imperial decree. Consequently, most recipes using meat date from just the last hundred years and have their origins in Chinese or European cuisine, which influenced the Japanese. The characteristic Japanese touches are the use of soy sauce, mirin, miso, and sake for seasoning.

Even today, the Japanese seldom eat meat, and large meat roasts are relatively rare. Because beef is very expensive it is usually sold very thinly sliced, especially the tender cuts, such as fillet, which are required for traditional dishes such as beef simmered in soy sauce and sake. Although the look of the food is an essential consideration, the Japanese are very partial to beef marbled with fat, which adds flavor and helps to ensure that the different flavors of the ingredients blend harmoniously. Pork is cheaper than beef and is often used in its place. Since Buddhists are only forbidden to slaughter four-legged animals, poultry has long been highly valued by the Japanese. High in protein and low in calories, it is a popular choice for maintaining their healthy diet. Chickens are usually sold in portions, rather than whole.

Beef Cooked in Soy Sauce

Prepare ahead • Entrée **Sukiyaki** *Serves 4*

**1 cup vacuum-packed
firm fresh tofu
(see page 48)
6 oz. Japanese cellophane noodles
3 oz. shitake mushrooms
3 oz. enokitake (oyster) mushrooms
7 oz. shungiku
("chrysanthemum leaves")
or leaf spinach
14 oz. Chinese (Napa) cabbage
2 leeks • 1 carrot
1 lb. 5 oz. fillet steak, cut into slices
⅛th in. thick (see Note)
4 very fresh eggs
3 tbsp. beef suet or vegetable oil
For the sukiyaki sauce
½ cup Japanese soy sauce
½ cup mirin (sweet rice wine)
2 tbsp. sugar**

Preparation time: 1 hour

740 cal. per serving

1 Dip the tofu briefly in cold water. Drain and carefully pat dry. Cut the tofu into 16 cubes or triangles.

2 Precook the noodles for about 5 minutes in plenty of boiling water, then drain and reserve.

3 Remove the stalks of the shitake mushrooms and wipe them with a cloth. Leave half the mushrooms whole and cut the rest into triangles. Wash the enokitake mushrooms, trimming off the brown ends of the stalks. Reserve the mushrooms. Trim and wash the shungiku.

4 Trim and wash the Chinese cabbage and cut the leaves into pieces about 4 inches long. Bring a saucepan of water to a boil. Add the cabbage and blanch for about 5 minutes. Drain and press gently to remove most of the water.

5 Remove the wilted green leaves and roots from the leeks, then wash them thoroughly. Cut slightly diagonally into 3-in. pieces. Wash and peel the carrot and cut into slices. Cut the slices into decorative shapes, if wished.

6 Arrange the prepared ingredients and the steak attractively on separate plates, each with a fork or chopsticks beside them.

7 To make the sauces, bring the soy sauce, mirin, and sugar briefly to a boil in a saucepan. Transfer ⅔ cup of the liquid to a small tea or coffee pot. Add 4 tbsp. water to the remaining liquid and pour the diluted sauce into another pot.

8 Break a raw egg into each of four bowls, and whisk. Place one bowl in front of each place setting.

9 Preheat a hotplate or gas burner on the table with a sukiyaki pot (see Note), or use a heavy-based skillet. Melt the suet or heat the oil and briefly fry a few slices of meat, adding about half the undiluted sauce.

10 Add some of the vegetables and tofu. When the sauce comes to a boil, add some of the noodles and cook them with the tofu, meat, and vegetables for 6 or 8 minutes.

11 Let your guests serve themselves from the pan with chopsticks or a fork, dipping the meat and other ingredients briefly in the beaten egg before eating.

12 The rate at which meat, vegetables, and other ingredients are eaten and new ones added to the pot to cook, is completely up to you and your guests. It is quite in order to help yourself from the pan and add more pieces of meat. However, avoid putting too much in the pan at once. During cooking, keep topping up with sauces, alternating the undiluted and diluted sauces so that the flavor is not too intense.

Drink: Warm sake is the best drink to serve with sukiyaki.

Note: This method of cooking food at the table is especially popular in winter. Most families have a special sukiyaki pot for cooking this dish. Such pots are obtainable from Japanese food stores. However, a heavy-based skillet and a portable cooking stove can be used instead.

Ask your butcher to slice the steak for you, or if prefer to slice it yourself, leave it for a short time beforehand in the freezer, and it will be much easier to cut into thin slices.

Make sure you only use very fresh eggs from a reliable source for this recipe, to reduce any risk of salmonella.

Boiled Belly of Pork

Tonbara no nimono

Takes time • Appetizer
Serves 4

11 oz. pork belly
walnut-sized piece fresh ginger root
(about ½ ounce)
4-in. piece daikon (Japanese white
radish)
2 cups sake (Japanese rice wine)
¾ cup Japanese soy sauce
¾ cup sugar
leek rings for garnish (optional)

Preparation time: 30 minutes
(plus 3 hours cooking time)

500 cal. per serving

1 Cut the pork into 2-in. dice and bind the pieces with kitchen thread so that the meat does not fall apart while cooking. Place the meat in a flameproof casserole or a saucepan with 1 quart water and cook, uncovered, for about 10 minutes over medium heat.

2 Meanwhile, peel and finely grate the ginger and daikon. Place them in two separate small bowls.

3 Place the ginger, sake, soy sauce, and sugar in a saucepan or flameproof casserole with 7 tbsp. water. Drain the meat, add it to the casserole, and bring to a boil. Simmer, covered, over low heat for 3 hours.

4 Remove the thread from the meat and serve with the grated radish. Garnish with leek rings, if wished.

Drink: We recommend you serve warm sake with this dish.

Note: Boiled Belly of Pork is sometimes served with rice as a entrée.

Pork Shoulder with Salad

Butaniku no misoyaki

Easy • Entrée
Serves 4

4 tbsp. red miso (soybean paste •
see page 38)
2 tbsp. sugar
4 tbsp. sake (Japanese rice wine)
4 tbsp. dashi 2 (see page 28)
1 tbsp. Japanese soy sauce
7 oz. white cabbage
1 small cucumber
salt
1 large tomato
¼ cup shelled, unsalted peanuts
1 tbsp. vegetable oil
1 lb. 5 oz. pork shoulder,
cut into slices ⅛ in. thick
freshly ground black pepper

Preparation time: 35 minutes
(plus 30 minutes for making the
dashi)

570 cal. per serving

1 Mix the miso, sugar, sake, and dashi. Heat through in a saucepan, stirring constantly. Do not allow the mixture to boil. Add the soy sauce, and set aside.

2 Trim and wash the white cabbage, and cut it into thin strips about ⅛ in. wide. To keep the cabbage crisp, leave it in cold water until ready to serve.

3 Wash the cucumber, rub it with salt, then rinse away the salt. If a decorative pattern is preferred, cut away strips of the skin along the whole length of the cucumber, using a lemon zester. Cut the cucumber diagonally into slices about ¾ in. thick.

4 Wash the tomato and cut it into eight wedges. Lightly toast the peanuts in a nonstick skillet, then remove them from the pan and chop coarsely.

5 Heat the skillet and add the oil. Lightly season the pork slices with salt and pepper. Fry the meat over medium heat for about 2 minutes. Remove the meat from the pan and spread with the miso sauce.

6 Peel the tomato wedges, leaving the skin attached at the end. Drain the cabbage and arrange it with the tomato and cucumber on four individual plates. Place the meat on top and sprinkle with the toasted chopped peanuts.

Drinks: Serve sake or Japanese beer with this dish.

Note: Rubbing the cucumber skin with salt gives it a brighter color and also cleans the skin.

Duck Teriyaki

Quick • Appetizer **Kamo no teriyaki** *Serves 4*

*14 oz. duck breast fillet,
with skin*
2 thin baby leeks
4 tbsp. sake (Japanese rice wine)
4 tbsp. mirin (sweet rice wine)
2 heaping tbsp. sugar
5 tbsp. Japanese soy sauce
1 tbsp. vegetable oil for frying
salt
hot mustard
*radishes and carrots carved into
decorative shapes for garnish
(optional)*

Preparation time: 30 minutes

330cal. per serving

1 Carefully make three incisions in the duck skin at right angles to the fibers of the meat. Trim the wilted green leaves and roots from the leeks, then wash the leeks and cut into 1-in. pieces.

2 In a nonstick skillet without fat, fry the duck, skin side downward, over high heat for about 3 minutes. Turn and fry for another 1 minute. Remove the duck from the pan and discard the fat.

3 In the same skillet, bring the sake, mirin, and sugar to a boil over medium heat. Add the duck, cover and cook for about 2 minutes, then add the soy sauce and turn the meat. Cover and cook for about 3 minutes, or until the sauce thickens, turning the meat from time to time. Discard the sauce.

4 In a second skillet, heat the oil and fry the leeks over medium heat for 2 to

3 minutes, until browned on all sides, then season to taste with salt.

5 Carved the cooked meat into slices about ¼ in. thick. Serve on individual plates with the leeks and a small dab of mustard. Garnish each portion with some of the decorative radishes and carrots, if using.

Variation: Boiled duck
Cut 8 oz. duck breast, with skin, into slices ¼ in. thick. Season with salt and pepper, coat in 2 tbsp. potato starch, then blanch in boiling water for about 1 minute. In a saucepan, bring 10 tbsp. mirin and 3 tbsp. soy sauce to a boil. Cook the duck in the sauce for about 30 seconds, or until medium-done. Drain the duck and return the sauce to a boil. Serve the duck with the hot sauce.

Chicken Kabobs

Quick • Appetizer **Yakitori** *Serves 4*

14 oz. boned chicken legs
2 thin leeks
¾ cup chicken broth (can be made with a bouillon cube)
½ cup Japanese soy sauce
3 tbsp. sugar
decoratively carved carrot slices and shiso leaves (see Glossary) or fresh herbs for garnish (optional)

Preparation time: 30 minutes

210 cal. per serving

1 If using a charcoal grill, preheat it before you start the preparation. If you are cooking on a table grill, preheat it before Step 3.

2 Cut the chicken into 1-in. dice. Trim the wilted green leaves and roots from the leeks, then cut each leek into eight equal-sized pieces.

3 Soak eight bamboo skewers in water for a few minutes, so that they do not burn on the grill. Bring the chicken broth, soy sauce, and sugar briefly to a boil in a saucepan over high heat.

4 Beginning with chicken, thread three pieces of chicken and two pieces of leek close together on each skewer.

5 Dip the skewers in the sauce, drain, then grill them over charcoal or on a table grill for 3 to 4 minutes on each

side, until the chicken and leek pieces have browned. (If necessary, you can brown them in a skillet, adding a little oil, before cooking them on the grill.) Brush the pieces with more sauce while they are grilling.

6 Arrange the skewers on four rectangular dishes and garnish with sliced carrots and shiso leaves, if using.

Drink: A cold beer is the best drink to serve with this dish.

Note: Serve the skewers with seven-spice mixture (see Glossary), so that those who like their food hot and spicy can season to taste. Vegetables, meats, variety meats, and seafood can also be prepared in this way. If you prefer, you can serve the skewers on one communal plate.

Chicken Teriyaki

Easy • Entrée   **Toriniku no nabe-teriyaki**   *Serves 4*

1 tbsp. vegetable oil
3 chicken breast fillets, with skin
(about 1⅓ lb.)
1 tbsp. sake (Japanese rice wine)
4 tbsp. Japanese soy sauce
4 tbsp. mirin (sweet rice wine)
2 tbsp. sugar
6 oz. white cabbage
about ½ cup each of finely grated
carrot, cucumber, and Japanese
cress for garnish (optional)

Preparation time: 30 minutes

240 cal. per serving

1 Heat the oil in a skillet. Place the chicken breasts in the pan, skin side down, and fry over medium heat for about 5 minutes. Turn the meat, cover the pan, and fry for a further 5 minutes, until crisp, shaking the pan frequently.

2 Remove the chicken from the pan and discard the oil. In the same skillet, bring the sake, soy sauce, mirin, and sugar to a boil.

3 Return the chicken to the pan, skin side upward, and simmer in the sauce over low heat for about 5 minutes, or until completely cooked through.

4 Trim, wash, and finely shred the white cabbage. Remove the meat from the sauce. Cut into slices about ½ in. thick.

5 Arrange the meat on four individual plates and serve garnished with the white cabbage. Add the grated carrot, cucumber, and cress as an additional garnish, if wished.

Note: Teriyaki is a very popular cooking style in Japan; its name derives from teri, meaning "shine" and yaki, which means "to grill." The name stays the same, even the chicken is fried or broiled rather than grilled.

Mirin

This sweet fermented low-alcohol rice wine is used exclusively for cooking, and is employed to give a subtle sweetness to many Japanese dishes. It is believed to have originated from Korea or southern China, though some claim that it was brought to Japan by European missionaries in the 16th century.

Mirin is made by a very complex process. First, a culture is added to boiled rice and left for two days to create a dry must. Glutinous rice and distilled alcohol are then added to it. The must is then left to mature for two months at a temperature of 25°C/77°F, at the end of which time the liquid is pasteurized, filtered, and bottled. It was soon realized that mirin could be used in cooking as a sugar substitute, and that it would also help to keep food fresh for longer.

This combination of alcohol and natural sweetness lends an inimitable Japanese "edge" to a variety of dishes. The slightly syrupy consistency gives a fine, shiny glaze to grilled and broiled foods, making them look especially appetizing. It also adds a subtle sweetness to sauces without being cloying. A good substitute is pale dry sherry, but it should be used more sparingly than the amounts of mirin called for in the recipes.

Chicken with Soy Sauce

Quick • Appetizer **Mushidori no yagarashi sosu kake** *Serves 4*

14 oz. chicken legs
3 tbsp. Japanese soy sauce
2 tbsp. mirin (sweet rice wine)
2 tbsp. sake (Japanese rice wine)
1 tbsp. sugar
2-in. piece fresh ginger root
8 iceberg lettuce leaves
1 small piece cucumber
2 tbsp. hot mustard

Preparation time: 30 minutes

150 cal. per serving

1 Using a very sharp knife, cut along the bone on both sides of each chicken leg, to detach the flesh from the bone (*above*). Pull each of the bones free and remove it.

2 Using a fork, pierce the skin on each of the chicken legs and then briefly dip them in a bowl of hot water. Rinse in cold water and leave to drain.

3 Line a flameproof casserole or large saucepan with enough aluminum foil to wrap over the chicken. Mix the soy sauce, mirin, sake, and sugar and pour half of it over the foil. Add the ginger and spoon the remaining sauce over the top. Close the foil to make a package.

4 Cover the casserole or pan and heat the chicken and soy sauce mixture for about 8 minutes over high heat, or until it begins to steam. As soon as the steam rises, reduce the temperature. Open the foil and turn the chicken legs over. Close

the foil again and steam the parcel over medium heat for a further 8 minutes. Leave the chicken to cool in the casserole or pan.

5 Wash and drain the lettuce and cut it into thin strips. Make incisions in the cucumber, without cutting all the way through, so that the flesh fans out. Cut the carrot into thin matchsticks.

6 Remove the chicken from the foil and slice thinly. Discard the ginger. Strain the sauce through a sieve and stir in the mustard.

7 Arrange the chicken on individual plates with the lettuce. Garnish with cucumber fans and carrot matchsticks. Pour the sauce over the chicken just before serving.

Drink: Japanese green tea goes best with this dish.

Variation: Grilled chicken
In a bowl, mix 2 tbsp. Japanese soy sauce, 2 tbsp. mirin, 1 tsp. sake, 1 tsp. rice vinegar (su), 1 tbsp. dashi 1 (see page 28) or chicken broth, 1 tsp. sugar. 1 tsp. lemon juice, and 1 tsp. toasted sesame seeds. Prepare the chicken as described in Step 1, then add it to the marinade in the bowl. Cover and leave to marinate in a cool place for at least 3 hours. Precook the chicken at 325 degrees in the center of the oven for about 15 minutes, spreading the marinade over it from time to time. Finish the cooking by broiling the chicken for about 5 minutes on each side under a broiler, or grill it over a charcoal grill or on a table grill.

Marinated Duck

Kamoniku no yakizuke

Prepare in advance • Appetizer Serves 4

8 oz. duck breast fillet
with skin
salt
freshly ground black pepper
2 thin leeks
7 tbsp. sake (Japanese rice wine)
5 tbsp. mirin (sweet rice wine)
7 tbsp. Japanese soy sauce
1 tbsp. vegetable oil
Decoratively carved carrot slices for
garnish (optional)

Preparation time: 20 minutes
(plus at least 2 hours marinating
time)

220 cal. per serving

1 Season the duck breast fillet with salt and pepper. Trim the wilted green leaves and roots from the leeks, wash them, cut into 1-in. pieces, then cut the pieces in half lengthwise.

2 To make the marinade, bring the sake, mirin, and soy sauce briefly to a boil in a saucepan over high heat, then pour into a bowl and leave to cool.

3 Lightly brush a skillet with oil and fry the duck fillet, skin side downward, over medium heat, for about 5 minutes. Turn the meat over and fry on the other side for a further 5 minutes, until crisp at the edge and still pink in the middle.

4 Brush the pan again with oil, add the leeks, and fry over medium heat for about 30 seconds.

5 Allow the meat and leeks to cool for about 15 minutes, then add them to the marinade. Cover and leave to marinate in the refrigerator for at least 2 hours, or preferably overnight.

6 Remove the meat and leeks from the marinade. Carve the meat into slices about ¼ in. thick. Strain the sauce through a sieve. Divide the meat between four plates, arranging the leeks around the edge so that they overlap. Pour the sauce over the duck before serving. Garnish with decoratively carved carrot slices, if wished.

Note: If you prefer a milder sauce, use 2 or 3 tbsp. less soy sauce.

Chilled Entrecôte Steak

Takes time • Appetizer **Gyuniku no tataki-fu** *Serves 4*

1 lb. entrecôte steak
3 garlic cloves
1 walnut-sized piece fresh ginger
root (about ½ ounce)
¾ cup Japanese soy sauce
4 tbsp. sake (Japanese rice wine)
½ daikon (Japanese white radish)
1 small cucumber
1 tbsp. vegetable oil

For serving:
wasabi (Japanese green
horseradish)
Japanese soy sauce

Preparation time: 30 minutes
(plus 3 hours marinating time and
1 hours chilling time)

170 cal. per serving

1 Cut the entrecôte steak into strips about 1 in. wide. Peel the garlic. Peel and finely grate the ginger. Stir the ginger, soy sauce, and sake together in a bowl. Crush the garlic and add it to the bowl. Add the meat to the mixture, cover, and leave to marinate in the refrigerator for about 3 hours.

2 Peel and thinly slice the daikon. Cut the slices into very thin shreds. Wash the cucumber, cut in half lengthwise, and then slice thinly.

3 Brush a skillet with oil. When the pan is hot, fry the steak strips for about 2 minutes, until browned all over. It should be still almost raw inside.

Dip the meat briefly in ice-cold water, then pat dry on paper towels. Leave it to chill in the refrigerator for about 1 hour, then cut into slices ¼ in. thick.

4 Arrange the meat in fan shapes on four individual plates, with the daikon, cucumber, and a blob of wasabi on top. Serve the meat with the soy sauce as a dip in a separate bowl.

Boiled Beef

Easy • Entrée

Gyuniku no yanagawa-fu

Serves 4

1 small burdock or salsify
1 tsp. rice vinegar (su)
1 tbsp. mirin (sweet rice wine)
¾ cup dashi 2 (see page 28)
3 tbsp. Japanese soy sauce
1 tbsp. sugar
8 oz. entrecôte steak, cut into slices about ⅛ in. thick
4 very fresh eggs
4 shiso leaves (see Glossary) or fresh herb leaves
decoratively carved carrot slices for garnish (optional)

Preparation time: 30 minutes (plus 30 minutes for making the dashi)

260 cal. per serving

1 Preheat the oven to its minimum setting. Wash and peel the burdock and cut into slices about ⅛ in. thick. Lay the burdock in a bowl with about 1 cup water and the vinegar, so that the burdock turns a lighter color.

2 Heat the mirin, dashi, soy sauce, and sugar in a saucepan, stirring to mix well. When the liquid comes to a boil, add the sliced meat and cook over medium heat for 1 to 2 minutes, or until the meat turns color. Remove the meat from the pan and keep it warm in the oven.

3 Remove the burdock from the water and add to the sauce in the pan. Cook for about 20 minutes, or until the burdock is tender, topping up with water from time to time. Return the sliced meat to the pan and heat through.

4 Serve the meat and burdock piping hot on four individual plates. Whisk the eggs and pour them over the meat. Garnish each portion with a shiso leaf and decorative carrot slices.

Note: Burdock, known in Japan as *gobo*, is a long, slender root vegetable with a brown skin and grayish-white flesh. It has a sweet, earthy flavor and crunchy texture. It is available fresh or canned from Japanese stores. Salsify (oyster plant) can be used instead in this recipe if burdock is unavailable.

Make sure you use only very fresh eggs from a reliable source, to reduce any risk of salmonella.

Deep-fried Chicken Legs

Quick • Entrée

Torinuku no kara-age

Serves 4

1 lb. 5 oz. chicken legs
4 tbsp. sake (Japanese rice wine)
2 tbsp. mirin (sweet rice wine)
2 tbsp. Japanese soy sauce
rice flour for sprinkling
1 quart vegetable oil for deep-frying
2 untreated lemons
lettuce leaves for serving

Preparation time: 30 minutes

670 cal. per serving

1 Pierce the skin of the chicken legs. Using a very sharp knife, cut along the bone on both sides of each chicken joint, to detach the flesh from the bone. Pull the bones free and remove them. Remove any surplus fat. Cut the meat into ¾-in. dice.

2 Mix the sake, mirin, and soy sauce in a bowl, add the diced meat, and leave to marinate for about 15 minutes. Drain the meat and sprinkle it with rice flour, turning and tapping the chicken pieces to remove any surplus flour.

3 Heat the oil in a heavy-based skillet until bubbles rise when you dip a wooden chopstick in it. If you are using an electric deep-fryer, preheat it to 350 degrees. Fry the chicken pieces in small batches for about 2 minutes, until crisp. Take care, the oil may spit! Drain off the oil, then lay the chicken briefly on paper towels to remove any remaining fat before serving.

4 Wash and quarter the lemons. Wash the lettuce leaves. Serve the chicken on the lettuce leaves on individual plates, accompanied by the lemon wedges.

Note: Season at the table with a little seven-spice mixture (see Glossary), if you prefer a hot and spicy flavor.

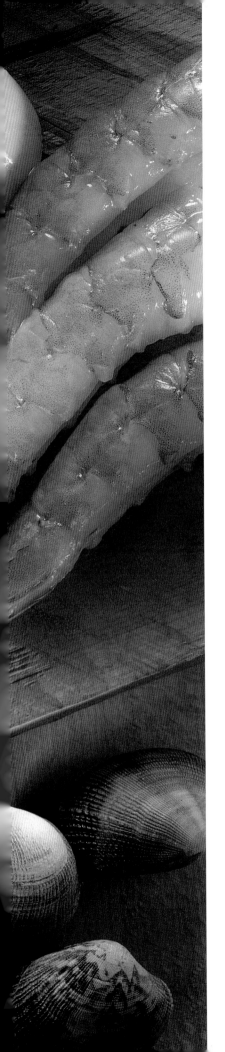

FISH, SUSHI, AND SASHIMI

A long with rice, fish is one of Japan's staple foods, eaten almost daily. It is far more than just a staple, though, for the many inventive dishes – most famously those using raw fish – are among the most delectable and decorative in the world.

The most important factor in the preparation of raw fish dishes such as sushi and sashimi is absolute freshness – frozen fish cannot be used. Indeed, Japanese restaurants often keep their fish for shashimi alive in tanks until the moment the customer orders it.

To enjoy raw fish to the full it is vital to buy only the best quality. Look for specimens whose skin has a natural shine, and which are not bruised or damaged in any way. Check the eyes, which should be crystal clear, not cloudy, if the fish is fresh. The gills should be bright red; if the fish is not fresh, the gills turn whitish and the fish will have begun to smell. Test the fish by pressing and sniffing it. Fresh fish is firm to the touch and smells of the sea. All fish and seafood should be kept refrigerated until ready for use, and should be handled as little as possible.

Some fish may carry parasites which can cause gastro-intestinal upsets, but given the number of people that eat it, the risk is a small one.

Raw Fish Fillets

Sashimi

3½ oz. tuna fillet,
in a square piece
no more than 1 in. thick
2 oz. salmon fillet
2½ oz. squid
2½ oz. turbot fillet
1 thick daikon
(Japanese white radish)
1 heaping tbsp. wasabi
(Japanese green horseradish)
sliced lime and decoratively carved
radishes and carrot slices for
garnish (optional)

For serving:
Japanese soy sauce
Preparation time: 1 hour

120 cal. per serving

1 Flat cut (hira giri):
Cut the tuna fillet in half. Take one half of the fillet, hold it carefully and firmly, then, with a very sharp knife, cut it vertically into slices about ¼ in. thick, cutting as if you were slicing a loaf of bread. Slice the entire salmon fillet in the same way.

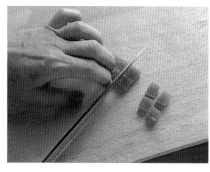

2 Cube cut (kaku giri):
Cut the other half of the tuna fillet into long slices about ½ in. wide. Take two slices at a time and cut them crosswise into ½ to ¾ in. cubes (*above*).

5 Peel the daikon. Trim the ends to make one piece about 4 inches long and the same thickness all the way down.

6 Using a very sharp knife, pare the daikon into a thin spiral (*below*). Cut the spiral into threads, or if you prefer, finely shred or grate the daikon.

3 Thread shape (ito giri):
Cut the squid crosswise into 1-in. slices and then cut lengthwise into thin strips about ⅛ in. wide (*above*).

4 Paper-thin slices (usi giri):
Lay the turbot flat on a chopping board and slice it at a slight angle into very thin, almost transparent sheets, using a very sharp knife (above, right).

7 Make the wasabi into a leaf shape and place it on the edge of a serving dish. Arrange the pieces of fish and daikon in an attractive pattern on the dish. Garnish with slices of lime, radish, and carrot, if using. Provide each person with a small bowl of Japanese soy sauce for dipping.

Note: To eat sashimi, put a little of the wasabi into the soy sauce and stir it in. Dip the fish into the sauce before eating.

Broiled Salmon

Easy • Entrée   **Sake no yuan-yaki**   *Serves 4*

1 yuzu or lime
5 to 6 tbsp. Japanese soy sauce
5 to 6 tbsp. mirin (sweet rice wine)
5 to 6 tbsp. sake (Japanese rice wine)
8 x 2-oz. slices salmon fillet
4 slices canned or frozen lotus root
salt
4 tbsp. rice vinegar
1 tbsp. sugar
decoratively carved carrot slices (optional)

Preparation time: 30 minutes (plus 2 hours marinating time)

290 cal. per serving

1 Rinse the yuzu or lime in hot water and slice into four pieces.

2 To make the marinade, mix the soy sauce, mirin, sake and yuzu in a dish. Add the salmon fillet slices, cover the dish, and leave the salmon to marinate in the refrigerator for about 2 hours.

3 Meanwhile, cook the lotus root in a pan of boiling salted water for about 2 minutes. Drain and, if necessary, cut crosswise into slices about ⅛ in. thick.

4 Mix the rice vinegar and sugar with 4 tbsp. water in a bowl, add the lotus root and leave to soak for 1 hour. After 50 minutes, preheat the broiler to high.

5 Remove the salmon slices from the marinade and place them on a greased broiler pan. Cook under the hot broiler for about 3 minutes, then turn the slices over and broil for a further 1 minute. Brush with the marinade from time to time while grilling.

6 Serve two salmon fillets per person, accompanied by the drained lotus root. Garnish each portion with decoratively carved carrots, if using.

Variation: Prepare 4 oz. salmon fillet per person, as described above. Peel, finely grate and then drain ½ daikon (Japanese white radish). Place a little pile of the grated daikon beside each portion of salmon. Sprinkle the salmon with soy sauce before eating. The daikon and salmon are eaten together.

Fried Fillet of Herring

Easy • Entrée   **Nishin no kara-age**   ***Serves 4***

4 herring fillets, with skin (about
3 oz. each)
2 tbsp. Japanese soy sauce
7 tbsp. sake (Japanese rice wine)
1 tbsp. all-purpose flour
1 tbsp. potato starch
1 quart vegetable oil for deep-frying
1 untreated lemon
Decoratively carved pieces of
cucumber for garnish (optional)

Preparation time: 20 minutes
(plus 1 hour's marinating time)

230 cal. per serving

1 Cut the fish fillets crosswise into two or three pieces with a sharp knife and make shallow incisions in the skin.

2 Stir the soy sauce and sake together in a bowl. Place the fish in the mixture, cover, and leave to marinate in the refrigerator for about 1 hour.

3 Mix the wheat and potato starches in another bowl. Remove the fish from the marinade and coat with the mixed flour.

4 Heat the oil in a heavy-based skillet until bubbles rise when you dip a wooden chopstick in it. If you are using an electric deep-fryer, heat the oil to 350 degrees. Fry the fish fillets in the oil until crisp.

5 Wash the lemon and cut it into eight wedges. Serve the fish on individual plates, garnished with decorative cucumber slices, if using. Squeeze the lemon juice over the fish before eating.

Variation: Make a marinade from 2 tbsp. each of Japanese soy sauce, rice vinegar (su), sake, and water, 1 tbsp. each of mirin (sweet rice wine) and 1 tsp. sugar. Wash 1 dried chili pepper (see Glossary). Remove the seeds, cut into thin rings, and add to the marinade. Coat the fish with the flour mixture and deep-fry. Place the warm fish in the marinade and marinate in the refrigerator for about 12 hours.

Fried Flounder

Easy • Starter　**Karei no oroshi-ni**　　**Serves 4**

4 flounder fillets (about 3 oz. each)
walnut-sized piece fresh ginger root (about ½ ounce)
6 tbsp. sake • 2 tbsp. all-purpose flour
½ daikon (Japanese white radish)
¾ cup Dashi 2 (see page 28)
5 tbsp. mirin (sweet rice wine)
5 tbsp. Japanese soy sauce
1 tbsp. vegetable oil
Japanese cress for garnish

Preparation time: 30 minutes (plus 30 minutes for making the dashi)

160 cal. per serving

1 Cut the flounder into 2-in. pieces. Peel and finely grate the ginger and reserve the juice. Mix the juice with 1 tbsp. of the sake in a bowl.

2 Add the fish to the bowl with the ginger juice and sake, and marinate for about 10 minutes, then pat the fish dry with paper towels and coat with flour. Peel and finely grate the daikon, then drain in a sieve for a few minutes.

3 Put the grated ginger, dashi, mirin, soy sauce, and remaining sake in a saucepan and bring to a boil.

4 Meanwhile, in a skillet, heat the oil, add the flounder pieces, and fry over medium heat for 3 to 4 minutes, until golden-brown.

5 Arrange the cooked fish pieces on four individual plates. Shape the grated daikon into little balls and place them beside the fish on the plates. Pour the sauce over the fish and serve at once. Garnish each portion with the cress.

Drink: A cool beer is the perfect drink to serve with this dish.

Flounder with Vegetable

Takes time • Entrée

2 tsp. dried shiitake mushrooms
1 carrot
2 oz. onion
1 small green bell paper
1 green onion (scallion, white part only, about 4 inches long
2 tbsp. all-purpose flour
8 flounder fillets (about 2 oz. each)
6 tbsp. sake (Japanese rice wine)
3 tbsp. sugar
1 tbsp. Japanese soy sauce
1 tbsp. potato starch
1 tbsp. vegetable oil

Preparation time: 45 minutes (plus 3 hours for soaking the mushrooms)

220 cal. per serving

1 Soak the mushrooms in cold water for about 3 hours. Drain them, discard the stalks, and cut the mushroom caps into matchsticks.

2 Peel the carrots and onion. Slice the onion lengthwise into thin strips. Slice the carrots lengthwise. Cut the slices into pieces about 2 inches long, and then into thin strips. Wash and trim the bell pepper and cut into thin 2-in. strips. Wash the green onion (scallion) and cut it into thin strips about 2 inches long.

3 Dissolve the all-purpose flour in about 2 tbsp. water. Wash the flounder fillets, pat them dry, and dip them in the batter.

4 Mix the sake, sugar, and soy sauce in a saucepan. Bring the mixture to a boil,

then add the mushrooms and the carrot, onion, and bell pepper strips. Return to a boil, then remove the pan from the heat.

5 Using a hand whisk, beat the potato starch into the vegetable mixture and continue to stir until the sauce thickens. Keep warm over low heat.

6 Heat the oil in a skillet and fry the fillets over medium heat for about 2 minutes on each side, or until crisp.

7 Serve two flounder fillets on each plate. Spread the vegetable mixture over the fish and garnish each portion with the green onion (scallion).

Sushi Rice

Easy • Basic recipe   **Sushi gohan**   *Makes 3½ cups cooked rice (Serves 4)*

2 cups medium-grain California rice
For the seasoning sauce:
3 tbsp. rice vinegar (su)
2 tsp. salt
4 tsp. sugar
few drops Japanese soy sauce

Preparation time: 30 minutes

400 cal. per serving

1 Rinse the rice three or four times in a bowl, or until the water runs clear. Drain the rice. Place it in a saucepan with 2 cups water and bring to a boil.

2 Reduce the heat and simmer over low heat for about 20 minutes. Place a folded kitchen towel between the saucepan and the lid to absorb the steam.

3 Bring the rice vinegar, salt, sugar, and soy sauce briefly to a boil in an uncovered saucepan over high heat. Reduce the heat and stir the sauce until the sugar has dissolved, then leave to cool slightly.

4 Place the warm rice in a stoneware bowl or one made of unlacquered wood. Carefully stir the vinegar solution into the rice with a wooden spoon, taking care not to crush the grains. Leave the rice to cool before further use.

Note: Water and rice are used in a ratio of 1:1, since the seasoning sauce is added after cooking.
If you want to prepare a large quantity of sushi rice at once, you can stir it to make the moisture evaporate more quickly.

Soy Sauce

Soy sauce was invented in China more than 2,500 years ago. Buddhist teaching forbade the use of meat and fish sauces which had been customarily used as seasonings and, in their search for alternatives, people discovered that cooked soybeans made a tasty and tangy alternative. The sauce was introduced to Japan during the 8th century with the arrival of Buddhism, since which time it has played a major role.

Japanese soy sauce is made from soybeans, wheat (a Japanese addition), sea salt, and water. A dry must is produced by adding *koji* (the fungal culture *aspergillus soiae*), to a mixture of stewed soybeans and ground wheat. After about 45 hours, sea salt and spring water are added to make a liquid must known as moromi. This is left to mature or ferment for six months to develop the characteristic aroma, taste, and color. It is then refined to make a well-balanced sauce.

Soy sauce is as important to Japanese cuisine as salt is to Western cooking. It is used as a dip, as a seasoning for cooking liquids, and as an ingredient in marinades.

Make sure you use a soy sauce imported from Japan (often called shoyu) when cooking Japanese food. The heavier and saltier Chinese versions are not suitable.

Sushi Rice with Salmon

Sake to ikura no oyako-zushi

Takes time • Entrée   *Serves 4*

2 cups medium-grain California rice
8 oz. salmon fillet
salt
¾ cup rice vinegar (su)
Japanese cress for garnish
½ sheet nori seaweed (see page 31)
1 heaping tbsp. wasabi
(Japanese green horseradish)
3½ oz. keta (salmon roe)
1 heaping tbsp. pickled sliced ginger
12 cucumber slices

For the pancake:
2 eggs • sugar • salt
Japanese soy sauce

For the sushi vinegar:
4 tbsp. rice vinegar
2 tbsp. sugar • 1 tbsp. salt
few drops Japanese soy sauce

Preparation time: 45 minutes
(plus 45 minutes' standing time)

740 cal. per serving

1 Rinse the rice three or four times in a bowl, until the water runs clear. Drain the rice. Place it in a saucepan with 2 cups water and bring to a boil.

2 Reduce the heat and simmer over low heat for about 20 minutes. Place a folded kitchen towel between the saucepan and the lid to absorb the steam.

3 Meanwhile, sprinkle the salmon fillet with salt, cover, and leave to stand in the refrigerator for about 30 minutes. Then place the salmon in a small bowl with enough rice vinegar to cover it completely. After about 15 minutes,

when the surface of the salmon has turned white, remove the fish from the bowl and wipe off any remaining vinegar.

4 To make the pancake, mix the eggs with a little sugar, salt, and soy sauce. Spread the mixture very thinly in a nonstick skillet and fry over medium heat to make a very thin pancake. Cut it into thin strips.

5 To make the sushi vinegar, mix the rice vinegar, sugar, salt, and soy sauce. Place the still-warm rice in a large bowl. Pour the mixture evenly over the rice. Stir with a large wooden spoon, taking care not to crush the grains.

6 Cut the salmon into strips about ⅛ in. thick. Rinse the daikon leaves and cut them into pieces 2-inch. Cut the seaweed into thin strips about 2 inches long. Press the wasabi flat and cut with a knife into a leaf shape.

7 Divide the rice between four bowls or soup plates. Arrange the sliced salmon in a circular pattern on top as if you were covering a cake. Place the keta in the center, surrounded by the cress, ginger, cucumber slices, and wasabi. Sprinkle with the seaweed and pancake strips.

Drink: A cool Japanese beer or green tea goes well with this refreshing dish.

Variation: Prepare the rice and pancake as described. Soak 4 dried shiitake mushrooms in 1¼ cups lukewarm water for about 20 minutes.

Discard the stalks, then place the mushrooms in a saucepan with ¾ cup of the water in which they have been soaked, and 1 tbsp. each of mirin (sweet rice wine), Japanese soy sauce, and sugar. Cover and simmer over low heat for about 20 minutes. Drain the mushrooms and cut them first into slices and then into thin strips. Thinly slice
2 oz. peeled fresh or frozen lotus roots. Cook them for about 5 minutes in water to which a dash of vinegar has been added, then marinate them in 1 tbsp. rice vinegar (su) and 1 tbsp. dashi 1 (see page 28) for 30 minutes. Peel and halve 1 oz. carrots, then slice them lengthwise. Cook the carrots for

about 3 minutes in 7 tbsp. dashi, with 1 tsp. sugar and a little soy sauce added. Peel and remove the heads and intestines from 16 oz. bay shrimp and boil them for about 1 minute, then marinate them in 1 tsp. wine vinegar, 1 tsp. sugar, and a little salt for 30 minutes, Blanch ½ cup sugar snap peas, then cut them into thin strips. Stir two thirds of the mushrooms, lotus roots, and carrots into the rice. Serve the rice in individual bowls, garnished with the rest of the ingredients and the pancake strips.

Note: 2 cups uncooked rice produces about 4 cups cooked sushi rice.

Rice in Seaweed

Easy • Entrée **Maki-zushi** *Makes about 48 (Serves 4)*

4 oz. fresh tuna fish fillet
1 small cucumber
4 sheets nori seaweed (see page 31)
3 cups prepared sushi rice (see page 106)
1 heaping tbsp. wasabi (Japanese green horseseradish)
3 ½ oz. pickled Japanese ginger

For serving:
Japanese soy sauce

Preparation time: 40 minutes (plus 30 minutes for preparing the sushi rice)

40 cal. per sushi

1 Using a sharp knife, cut the fresh tuna fillet into strips ½ in. wide and about 2 inches long.

2 Wash and peel the cucumber, cut it in half lengthwise, and scrape out the seeds with a teaspoon. Cut the halves crosswise into pieces about 2 inches long, then lengthwise into strips ¼ in. wide.

3 Using kitchen scissors, carefully cut the sheets of seaweed in half crosswise. Lay them flat on a bamboo rolling mat.

4 Lay half a sheet of seaweed on the mat and spread it with a layer of sushi rice about ¼ in. deep, leaving ½ in. uncovered at the top edge (*above*).

5 Working from right to left and using your fingers, lightly sprinkle a layer of wasabi across the middle (*above*), then place either a strip of tuna fish or three slices of cucumber on top.

6 Starting at the bottom edge, where the rice is, roll up the seaweed, using the bamboo mat, so that the rice roll is rectangular. Roll it carefully to avoid splitting the seaweed, then gently squeeze the roll.

7 Remove the bamboo mat and repeat the process until all the seaweed sheets are used up. Hold a sharp knife under cold water and then cut each roll into six rounds of equal size.

8 Drain the pickled ginger. Serve each person with about six pieces of each of the tuna and cucumber sushi, arranged on a plate with the rice side upward, with a few slices of ginger on the side. Serve soy sauce as a dip.

Note: If you are serving these sushi in a meal with rice and fish sushi (see page 113), serve seven of the "sandwiches" to four of the "rolls."

Rice and Fish Sushi

More complicated • Entrée   **Nigri-zushi**   *Makes about 40 (Serves 4)*

4 oz. each tuna, mackerel,
salmon, bass, and turbot fillet
2 heaping tbsp. wasabi
(Japanese green horseradish)
3 ½ cups prepared sushi rice (see
page 106)
4 oz. pickled Japanese ginger
leaves, flowers, chives and
decoratively carved carrot slices for
garnish (optional)

For serving:
Japanese soy sauce

Preparation time: 1 hour
(plus 30 minutes for preparing the
sushi rice)

67 cal. per sandwich

1 With a very sharp knife, cut the tuna, mackerel, salmon, bass, and turbot into slices about 1/4 in. wide, and then into rectangles about 1 in. wide and 2 inches long (*above*).

2 Using your finger, smear a piece of fish with a little wasabi. Repeat with all the pieces (*above*).

3 Moisten your hands, then roll the sushi rice into croquettes about 2 inches long and 1 in. in diameter. Place a rice croquette on a piece of fish, laying it on top of the wasabi (*above*). Press firmly so that the rice and the fish

stick together. Repeat the process until all the pieces of fish and all the croquettes have been used.

4 Drain the pickled ginger. Arrange about 10 sushi per person on a serving dish, with a little pile of pickled ginger on the side.

5 Garnish each portion with leaves, flowers, chives, and decoratively carved carrot slices, as desired. Serve a small bowl of Japanese soy sauce as a dip.

Drink: Traditionally, Japanese green tea is served with sushi.

Note: Since it contains rice, sushi is eaten as an entrée in Japan.
It is best to order the fish in advance from your fishmonger. You can cook the sushi rice beforehand, but you should only cut the fish shortly before serving, so that it does not dry out.
Sushi can be eaten with the fingers or with chopsticks. Before eating, briefly dip the sushi in soy sauce, fish downward, so that the rice does not fall apart. A little ginger should be eaten at intervals to clean the palate.

Rice with Tuna

More difficult • Entrée

Maguro gohan

Serves 4

1¾ cups medium-grain California rice
7 tbsp. sesame seeds
4 tbsp. Japanese soy sauce
1 heaping tsp. wasabi (Japanese
green horseradish)
14 oz. very fresh tuna fillet
½ sheet nori seaweed (see page 31)
Japanese cress for garnish

Preparation time: 45 minutes

740 cal. per serving

1 Rinse the rice three or four times in a bowl, or until the water runs clear. Drain the rice. Place it in a saucepan with 2½ cups water and bring to a boil.

2 Reduce the heat and simmer over low heat for about 25 minutes. Place a folded kitchen towel between the saucepan and the lid to absorb the steam.

3 Meanwhile, using a pestle and mortar, grind the sesame seeds to a paste to release the oil. Mix the paste with the soy sauce and wasabi.

4 Cut the tuna into slices ¼ in. thick. Using kitchen scissors, cut the seaweed into thin strips.

5 Divide the cooked rice between four rice bowls and sprinkle it with the strips of seaweed. Smear one side of the tuna slices with sesame paste and arrange them on top of the rice with the paste side downward. Sprinkle with cress and serve at once.

Drink: Green tea is the classic drink to serve with this dish.

Shrimp and Nori Rolls

Easy • Appetizer **Ebi narutomaki** *Serves 4*

10 unpeeled jumbo shrimp (about
1 oz. each)
1 cup mayonnaise
2 green onions (scallions), white
part only,
each about 4 inches long
4 sheets nori seaweed (see page 31)
3 tbsp. all-purpose flour
4 cups vegetable oil for deep frying
decoratively carved carrot slices
and cucumber pieces for garnish

For serving:
Japanese soy sauce

Preparation time: 30 minutes

860 cal. per serving

1 Wash and shell the shrimp and remove the heads and dark vein-like intestines (see Step 3, page 44). Dry the shrimp thoroughly and then grind them coarsely in a suribachi (Japanese ribbed grinding bowl) or blender. Stir in the mayonnaise.

2 Wash the green onions (scallions) and cut them into thin rings about $\frac{1}{32}$ in. wide.

3 Lay one sheet of nori on a bamboo rolling mat. Using a knife or dough scraper, spread the seaweed with a quarter of the shrimp mayonnaise, and sprinkle with the green onions (scallions). Roll up with the bamboo

mat, then remove the mat. Coat the roll with flour. Repeat the process three times more.

4 Heat the oil in a heavy-based saucepan until bubbles rise when you dip a wooden chopstick in it. If you are using an electric deep-fryer, heat the oil to 660° F. Deep-fry the rolls for about 2 minutes.

5 Drain the rolls and place them on paper towels to remove excess grease. Cut each roll straight or at a slight angle into about six rolls per person, with the Japanese soy sauce as a dip. Garnish each portion with decoratively carved carrot slices and cucumber.

Pickled Sardines

Takes time • Entrée **Iwashi no ume-ni** *Serves 4*

*14 oz. fresh sardines, cleaned
and ready to cook
salt
1 walnut-sized piece fresh ginger
½ in. piece kombu seaweed
(see page 31)
8 umeboshi (Japanese pickled
plums)
5 tbsp. sake (Japanese rice wine)
1 tbsp. sugar
4 tbsp. Japanese soy sauce
pickled kombu and shiso leaves
(see Glossary) for garnish (optional)*

*Preparation time: 40 minutes
(plus 12 hours for salting the
sardines)*

180 cal. per serving

1 Wash and dry the sardines. Sprinkle them with salt, cover, and leave to stand in the refrigerator overnight to draw off all the liquid.

2 Place the sardines in a colander and rinse them with hot water to remove the fishy smell.

3 Peel the ginger root and cut it into slices about ½ in. thick. Cut half the slices into thin matchsticks.

4 Place the seaweed and slices of ginger in a large saucepan. Arrange the sardines in the pan so that they do not overlap. Add the umeboshi.

5 Mix the sake, sugar and soy sauce with 4 tbsp. water, and pour the mixture over the sardines. Bring to a boil over medium heat and cook, uncovered, for 15 minutes, then turn the sardines over and cook for a further 15 minutes.

6 Divide the sardines between four individual plates, and serve with the ginger matchsticks and umeboshi. If wished, garnish with pickled seaweed and shiso leaves.

Note: Ginger root is an ingredient in many Japanese dishes. Really fresh ginger looks plump and unwrinkled. If you wrap it in a damp cloth, it will keep in the vegetable compartment of the refrigerator for about two weeks.

Marinated Tuna

Quick • Appetizer   **Maguro to negi no nuta**   *Serves 4*

3 ½ oz. very fresh tuna
1 tsp. salt
4 tbsp. rice vinegar (su)
4 green onions (scallions)
2 oz. wakame seaweed
(see page 31)
4 tbsp. white miso
(soybean paste • see page 38)
2 heaping tbsp. sugar
1 tsp. hot mustard
1 untreated lemon

Preparation time: 20 minutes

130 cal. per serving

1 Cut the fresh tuna into ½ in. cubes. Lightly season the fish cubes with salt and coat them with 2 tbsp. of the rice vinegar. Reserve the vinegar.

2 Wash and trim the green onions (scallions,) and cut them into rings about ½ in. wide. Blanch them in boiling water for about 1 minute, then drain.

3 Soak the seaweed in water for about 3 minutes. Drain off the water when the seaweed is still hard but pliable.

4 Rinse the green onions (scallions) and seaweed in the reserved vinegar – this improves the flavor – and then drain them.

5 Whisk the miso, sugar, mustard, and remaining vinegar in a bowl, using a hand whisk. Continue to whisk the mixture until the sugar has dissolved.

6 Wash the lemon thoroughly, and peel it. Cut the lemon rind into very thin strips about ¹⁄₃₂ in. wide.

7 Carefully stir the tuna, green onions (scallions) and seaweed into the sauce. Leave to stand for at least 3 minutes before serving in individual bowls, garnished with lemon rind.

Note: As the tuna is eaten raw, make sure that it is absolutely fresh.

Ocean Perch with Noodle Stuffing

More complicated • Entrée **Tai shinano-age** *Serves 4*

*2 thick ocean perch fillets (about
8 oz. each)*
salt
*1 green onion (scallion,) white part
only, about 4 inches long*
*3 ½ oz. chasoba noodles
(green soba noodles)*
potato starch for coating
2 oz. daikon (Japanese white radish)
2 cups dashi 1 (see page 28)
7 tbsp. mirin (sweet rice wine)
7 tbsp. Japanese soy sauce
1 quart vegetable oil for deep-frying

*Preparation time: 1 hour
(plus 1 hour for salting the fish and
15 minutes for making the dashi)*

710 cal. per serving

1 Clean the fish fillets, sprinkle them with salt, and leave to stand for about 1 hour. Meanwhile, wash and trim the green onion (scallion) and cut it into thin rings about ⅟₃₂ in. wide.

2 Make an incision about halfway through each fillet, then cut sideways into the flesh to make a pocket (*above*).

3 Divide the noodles into two bundles and tie with kitchen thread. Bring a saucepan of water to a boil and cook the noodles for 5 minutes. Drain them, rinse in cold water and leave to cool.

4 Remove the kitchen twine from the noodles. Stuff the fish generously with the noodles and carefully sew up with kitchen thread.

5 Coat the fish with potato starch. Peel and finely grate the daikon. Mix the radish, dashi, mirin and soy sauce in a saucepan, and bring briefly to a boil.

6 Heat the oil in a heavy-based saucepan until bubbles rise when you dip a wooden chopstick in it. Fry the fish in the oil for about 6 minutes, until golden-brown, then cut the fillets into 2-in. pieces.

7 Arrange the fish pieces in the soup bowls and pour over the daikon sauce. Garnish each portion with green onions (scallions).

Variation: Cold soba noodles
Cook and drain 14 oz. noodles, rinse them in cold water and drain again. To make the sauce, mix 2 tbsp. mirin, 1 ¾ cups dashi 1 and 3 tbsp. Japanese soy sauce and pour into four small pots. Prepare a small plate of wasabi (Japanese green horseradish) and green onions (scallions). Divide the cold noodles between four separate plates and garnish with nori seaweed (see page 31). When ready to eat, stir the nori and green onions (scallions) into the sauce. The noodles are eaten with chopsticks. Dip them briefly in the sauce before slurping down.

Mackerel with Miso

Quick • Appetizer **Saba no miso-ni** *Serves 4*

2 fresh mackerel fillets, with skin
(about 5 oz. each)
4 oz. white miso
(soybean paste • see page 38)
1-in. piece fresh ginger root
4 tbsp. sake (Japanese rice wine)
1 tbsp. sugar
1 umeboshi (Japanese pickled
plum • optional)
4 radishes, decoratively carved, if
wished

Preparation time: 30 minutes

220 cal. per serving

1 Wash the mackerel fillets and pat them dry with paper towel. Cut each fillet into three or four smaller pieces, making several incisions in the skin.

2 In a bowl, dissolve the miso in 1¼ cups water, using a hand whisk. Peel the piece of ginger root and cut it into two or three slices.

3 Pour the miso into a saucepan and add the sake, sugar, and ginger. Bring the mixture to a boil.

4 Turn the heat down low. Carefully add the mackerel fillets to the miso sauce, one at a time, making sure the pieces do not stick together. Pit and add the umeboshi, if using.

5 Cover the pan and cook the mackerel over low heat for about 15 minutes, until they have absorbed some of the miso sauce.

6 Discard the umeboshi. Wash the radishes. Arrange the mackerel fillets and the sauce on individual plates, and garnish each one with a radish.

Drink: A cool beer is the best drink to serve with this dish.

Note: You can prepare this dish with other types of fish, such as ocean perch.

Mackerel with Onions

Easy • Entrée　　**Saba no age-ni**　　　　　　　*Serves 4*

8 mackerel fillets, with skin (about 2 oz. each)
potato starch for coating
3 oz. onions
2 oz. daikon (Japanese white radish)
walnut-sized pieces fresh ginger
2 tbsp. vegetable oil
7 tbsp. dashi 2 (see page 28)
3 to 4 tbsp. mirin (sweet rice wine)
3 to 4 tbsp. Japanese soy sauce

Preparation time: 45 minutes (plus 15 minutes for making the dashi)

330 cal. per serving

1 Wash the mackerel fillets and pat them dry. Make several incisions on the skin side. Sift the potato starch into a shallow bowl and coat the mackerel fillets with the flour.

2 Peel the onions and cut them into thin rings. Peel and finely grate the daikon and ginger.

3 Heat the oil in a skillet and fry the mackerel for about 90 seconds, then turn them over and cook for a further 90 seconds.

4 Bring the dashi, mirin, and soy sauce to a boil in a large saucepan. Add the onion rings and mackerel fillets. Simmer, uncovered, over low heat for 10 to 15 minutes, turning the fish once.

5 Serve the mackerel and the sauce on individual plates with the grated daikon and ginger on the side.

Drink: Cool Japanese beer or sake is excellent with this hearty dish.

Note: Mackerel, which can be broiled, grilled, fried, or braised, is enjoyed throughout the world. Its high fat content of nearly 12 percent makes it a particularly good fish to smoke.

Clams in Sake

Simple • Appetizer   **Kai no sakamushi**   *Serves 4*

3 ½ cups clams in the shell
12 chives
1 walnut-sized piece fresh ginger
root (about ½ ounce)
¾ cup sake (Japanese rice wine)
2 tbsp. Japanese soy sauce

Preparation time: 15 minutes
(plus 2 hours for soaking the clams)

150 cal. per serving

1 Tap any clam shells that open and discard those that don't close. Soak the rest in cold, salted water for about 2 hours, changing the water if it becomes muddy, then wash and scrub thoroughly with a stiff brush.

2 Wash the chives and cut them into pieces ¼ in. long. Peel and finely chop the ginger.

3 Place the clams in a saucepan or a skillet with the sake, cover the pan, and cook over medium heat for about 5 minutes, then check to see whether the clams have opened. If they have not opened, cook for a further 2 minutes. When most of the clams are open, add the chives, chopped ginger, and soy sauce, and then shake the saucepan thoroughly – do not stir. Discard any clams that remain closed after cooking.

4 Pour the clams into four warmed bowls and serve at once.

Drink: As the clams are simmered in sake, the best accompaniment to serve with this dish is warm sake.

Note: Clams quickly become tough if they are overcooked, so make sure you remove the saucepan from the heat as soon as the shells open and the meat inside starts to swell.

Sake

Along with tea, sake is Japan's most famous and popular drink. It is made by fermenting rice and water and has an alcohol content of about 15 percent, similar to a strong grape wine. Although called rice wine, it is more closely related to beer.

Sake is a drunk during festivals and on other celebratory occasions. When it is to be drunk warm, it is poured into small flasks known as *tokkuri*, and heated in a bain-marie to about 126° F. The warmed sake is then served in beakers (*sakazuki*). For cold sake, glasses or square cedarwood cups are used. A little salt is placed in one corner of the cup, and the trick is to take a quick lick of the salt before drinking.

Sake is often used in cooking, and also for making marinades; it is good for removing saltiness, fishy flavor or any other strong tastes from foods.

Sake does not require any aging, and therefore no vintage year is indicated as it is with wine. In fact, it is best drunk as young as possible and, being a product of fermentation, should be stored in the dark.

Fish Teppanyaki

Easy • Entrée
Gyokai no teppanyaki

Serves 44

7 oz. each salmon and halibut fillet
7 oz. scallops, shells and coral removed
16 unpeeled, raw jumbo shrimp
2 onions • 1½ class mushrooms
1 large eggplant
¾ cup beansprouts
7 oz. broccoli
4 tbsp. vegetable oil

For the Pon-zu Sauce:
8 tbsp. yuzu juice or lemon juice
4 tbsp. Japanese soy sauce

For the sesame sauce:
4 tbsp. white sesame seeds
1 tbsp. white miso (soybean paste • see page 38)
2 tbsp. mirin (sweet rice wine)
2 tbsp. rice vinegar (su)
5 tbsp. Japanese soy sauce
1 tbsp. hot mustard

Preparation time: 40 minutes (cooked at the table)

450 cal. per serving

1 Wash and pat dry the salmon and halibut fillet and cut each fish into four equal-sized pieces.

2 Wash the scallops and pat them dry. Using your thumbs, break the shrimp shells on the underside. Wash and shell the shrimp, then make a shallow incision along the back of each shrimp and remove the dark vein-like intestine (see Step 3, page 44.)

3 Peel the onions and cut them into slices. Briefly rinse the mushrooms and pat them dry. Discard the mushroom stalks and cut the larger mushroom caps in half.

4 Wash and dry the eggplant, remove the stalk, cut it in half lengthwise and then into slices ¼ in. thick. Wash the beansprouts in a colander under cold running water, then drain them.

5 Wash the broccoli and separate into flowerets. Bring some water to a boil in a saucepan and blanch the broccoli for about 3 minutes, then drain, and rinse in cold water. Drain again.

6 Arrange the prepared fish, shellfish, and vegetables in an attractive pattern on a large serving platter, and set aside. Place a small electric hotplate or table grill on the table and preheat.

124

7 To make the Pon-zu Sauce, mix the yuzu or lemon juice and soy sauce in a bowl. To make the sesame sauce, grind the sesame seeds, using a pestle and mortar, then mix the ground seeds with the miso, mirin, rice vinegar, soy sauce, and mustard.

8 Pour the sauces into small individual bowls and place them in front of each of the table settings to use as dips with the cooked fish and vegetables.

9 Place a large cast iron skillet on the electric hotplate or table grill. Heat the oil in the pan and fry the fish and vegetables for about 6 minutes. Let everyone help themselves, dipping the fish and vegetables in either the Pon-zu or Sesame Sauce before eating.

Drink: As the atmosphere can become rather warm when using a hotplate or grill, it is best to serve cold Japanese beer with the dish.

Note: At family meals in Japan, it is usually the father who cooks the fish and vegetable teppanyaki at the table. Meat and other types of vegetables can also be prepared in the same way.

Gas burners for use at the table, fueled by gas cartridges, are available from stores specializing in oriental foods. These burners are also suitable for cooking outdoors.

SNACKS AND SWEETS

Japan has no lengthy tradition of dessert cooking, for it was only in the middle of the 8th century that sugar was first introduced to these islands from China. Even them, for hundreds of years this new gourmet food was largely reserved for the upper classes. Not until the late 19th century did its use become more widespread. Nonetheless, Japanese cakes, cookies, and sweet snacks are still very different from their Western counterparts, which use flour, eggs, and fat. Snacks here are usually combinations of local ingredients such as rice, seaweed, and adzuki beans. For example, it has recently become fashionable to serve ice cream with a warm adzuki bean sauce.

The usual way to finish a meal in Japan is with a light dessert such as fresh fruits in season. These include clementines, Asian or Japanese pears (*nashi*), persimmon (*kaki*) and the luscious homegrown strawberries that appear in February.

Green tea is traditionally served at the end of the meal, perhaps with some sweet jelly. Often, however, jelly is served at the beginning of a meal, when people meet in the late afternoon to take matcha, the bitter powdered tea that is used for the tea ceremony. The bitter tang of the tea provides a pleasant contrast to the intense sweetness of the jelly.

Sweet Rice Croquettes

O-hagi

Takes time • Traditional

Serves 4

¾ cup glutinous rice
1 ¾ cup canned cooked
adzuki beans (ogura an)

Preparation time: 1 ½ hours
(plus 12 hours for soaking the rice)

430 cal. per serving

1 Soak the glutinous rice in cold water for at least 12 hours or overnight. Rinse and drain through a fine sieve.

2 Fill a large saucepan with water to a level of about 2 inches. Suspend a colander or steamer attachment over the pan so that it does not touch the water. Line the colander or steamer with a kitchen towel and spread the rice on top. Bring the water to a boil. Cover the pan and steam the rice for about 30 minutes, until you can squash the individual grains between your fingers.

3 Transfer the rice to a container with a lid. Add ¾ cup hot water, cover and leave to stand for about 20 minutes, or until the rice has absorbed the water. Remove the rice from the container and leave to cool, wrapped in a damp cloth to prevent it hardening.

4 After about 20 minutes, moisten your hands and shape the cooled rice into croquettes about 2 inches long (*above*).

5 Pour the beans into a bowl and stir them gently with a wooden spatula to mash them to a thick paste. Take 1 tbsp. of the bean paste in your hand and spread it so that the palm of your hand is covered with beans (*above*).

6 Place a rice croquette on top of the beans (*above*) and then spoon another 1 tbsp. of the bean paste on top of the croquette. Squeeze the beans around the croquette so that the rice is completely covered.

Drink: Japanese green tea goes best with this sweetmeat.

Note: Glutinous rice (also known as sticky or sweet rice) is available from specialty food stores.

The rice croquettes look very pretty arranged on a plate with leaves and flowers, as here.

Deep-fried Rice Cakes

Quick • Easy   **Age-mochi**   *Serves 4*

1 quart vegetable oil for deep-frying
10½ oz. kiri mochi (Japanese rice
cakes, sold ready-made in
specialty food stores)
salt

Preparation time: 40 minutes

620 cal. per serving

1 Heat the oil in a heavy-based saucepan until bubbles rise when you dip a wooden chopstick in it. If you are using an electric deep-fryer, heat the oil to 350 degrees.

2 While the oil is heating, cut the kiri mochi into ½ in. cubes.

3 Gradually add the rice cake cubes to the hot fat and fry until golden. Take care, the fat may spit! As rice cakes swell considerably, do not put too many in the oil at once. They will turn over on their own as they cook. When they are ready, they will float to the surface.

4 Sprinkle the fried cakes with a little salt while they are still warm, then serve at once.

Note: At one time, Japanese families made their own rice cakes at home. Glutinous rice was boiled and then mashed to a pulp in a wooden trough using a wooden masher. The rice pulp was formed into round shapes and left to set before being cooked in the way described above.

Deep-fried rice cakes taste good warm or cold.

Stuffed Pancakes

Quick • Prepare in advance **Dora-yaki** *Serves 4 to6*

2 eggs
7 tbsp. milk
2 tbsp. sugar
2 tbsp. honey
1 cup all-purpose flour
1 tsp. baking powder
6 tbsp. canned cooked
adzuki beans (ogura an)

Preparation time: 30 minutes

290 cal. per serving

1 Using a hand whisk, thoroughly mix the eggs, milk, sugar and honey in a large mixing bowl.

2 Mix the flour and baking powder, and sift into a separate bowl.

3 Whisk the flour into the egg mixture adding a little at a time, to avoid lumps forming in the batter.

4 Place a nonstick skillet over medium heat and add 2 tbsp. of the batter. Tilt the pan so that the batter covers the base, then cook for about 2 minutes,

until air bubbles form on the surface. Turn the pancake with an egg slice and fry on the other side for about 3 minutes. Remove from the pan and keep warm while making another seven pancakes from the rest of the batter.

5 Briefly stir the adzuki beans and spread then over four of the pancakes. Top with the other four pancakes. Cut each one into four wedges and serve.

Drink: Serve Japanese green tea with these stuffed pancakes.

Chestnut Cakes

Easy • Takes time   **Kuri manjyu**   *Makes 8 (Serves 4)*

For the pastry:
7 oz. all-purpose flour
1 tbsp. fresh yeast
1 tsp. sugar
salt
1 ½ cups lukewarm milk
1 tsp. baking powder

For the filling:
⅔ cup sugar
¾ cup canned unsweetened chestnut purée
salt

Preparation time: 1 hour (plus 1 hour proving time)

430 cal. per serving

1 Sift the flour into a bowl and make a well in the center. Mix the yeast, sugar, salt, and 1 tbsp. water in the well. Cover and leave in a warm place to rise for about 10 minutes.

2 Add the milk and 2 tbsp. warm water, a little at a time. Working inward from the edge, knead the ingredients to a dough. Knead thoroughly, then cover the bowl and leave the dough to prove in a warm plate for about 1 hour.

3 Add the baking powder to the dough and knead again. Leave the dough in a warm place while making the filling.

4 To make the filling, place the sugar, chestnut purée, and a little salt in a saucepan. Heat through over medium heat, stirring constantly with a fork or dough hook, until all the liquid has evaporated and the purée begins to stiffen. Take care that it does not burn. Transfer the purée to a bowl and leave until it is completely cold.

5 Divide the dough into eight pieces and roll them out into eight circles. Place one ball of filling on each circle and wrap the dough round it (*above*).

6 Pour 3 cups of water into a large saucepan. Suspend a colander or steamer over the pan, making sure that it does not come into contact with the water. Line the colander or steamer with a cloth and arrange the cakes on the cloth.

7 Bring the water to a boil. Place a folded kitchen towel between the pan and the lid and briskly steam the cakes for about 8 minutes.

Note: Canned chestnut purée is available unsweetened or sweetened. The unsweetened purée is good for adding to stuffings and dressings to serve with roast meats, or for making sauces. The sweetened purée is very sweet and sticky, and can be mixed with cream or yogurt to make desserts and ice creams. It also combines beautifully with chocolate to make rich, irresistible desserts.

Variation: Chestnut cakes taste even better in fall, when you can make your own chestnut purée. To make them easier to shell, soak 1 lb. chestnuts in their shells in warm water for about 2 hours, preferably overnight. Boil the chestnuts over medium heat for about 40 minutes, until they are soft. Shell and mash them, season to taste with sugar and salt, then use as described in the recipe.

Adzuki Bean Jelly

Takes time • Light dessert   **Mizu yokan**   *Serves 4*

¼ oz. block of kanten
(agar-agar see Glossary)
⅔ cup sugar
salt
3 oz canned cooked adzuki beans
(ogura-an)
leaves and flowers for decoration
(optional)

**Preparation time: 30 minutes
(plus 30 minutes for soaking the
kanten and 1 hours cooling time)**

200 cal. per serving

1 Wash the kanten in water, tear it into small pieces and soak it in water for about 30 minutes, Pour off the water, squeeze the kanten and put it in a saucepan with ¾ cup water. Bring to a boil and boil until the kanten dissolves, stirring constantly.

2 Strain the liquid through a cloth into a saucepan and return it to a boil. Slowly stir in the sugar and a little salt. Continue to stir until the sugar has dissolved.

3 Slowly stir in the adzuki beans and cook over medium heat for about 2 minutes, stirring all the time to stop them burning. Remove from the heat and leave to cool to room temperature.

4 Moisten the inside of a rectangular mould with water. Pour the bean mixture into the mould and leave to set for at least 1 hour. Cut the jelly into pieces about 2 by 1 inch. Decorate with flowers and leaves, if using, and serve.

Drink: Matcha tea, which is used in the Japanese tea ceremony, is the perfect drink to serve with Adzuki Bean Jelly.

Variation: Omit the adzuki beans. Mix about 1 tbsp. matcha powder (Japanese powdered tea, which is available from specialty food stores) with the melted kanten. Increase the quantity of sugar to 1 cup and prepare the jelly as described above, omitting the beans.

Ice Cream with Bean Sauce

Quick • Light dessert   **Ogura aisu-kurimu**   *Serves 4*

¾ *cup canned cooked adzuki*
beans (ogura-an)
7 tbsp. heavy cream
4 strawberries
1 kiwi fruit
1 slice pineapple
12 small balls vanilla ice cream

Preparation time: 15 minutes

240 cal. per serving

1 Drain the canned adzuki beans in a sieve, then place them in a bowl, add the cream, and stir to mix.

2 Wash the strawberries and pat them dry. Cut them in half and then into decorative fan shapes. Peel the kiwi fruits and cut into slices about ⅛ in. thick. Cut the pineapple into eight pieces.

3 Place three balls of ice cream in each bowl. Top with the bean sauce and decorate with fruit.

Variation: Adzuki Bean Ice Cream
Whisk 2 egg yolks and 3 tbsp. sugar in a double saucepan or a heatproof bowl. Place it over a saucepan of simmering water over medium heat and cook until frothy. Stir in ¾ cup canned cooked adzuki beans. Pour the mixture into a freezer container and freeze for about 2 to 3 hours. Use a scoop to shape the ice cream into balls, and serve with fruit in season, such as kiwi fruits, strawberries, or Galia melon.

Note: You can buy canned adzuki beans in specialty food stores. In winter, warm adzuki bean sauce can be served with ice cream. Heat the beans and cream in a double saucepan or a heatproof bowl placed over a saucepan of simmering water.

Tofu balls

Easy • Snack   **Mitarashi dango**   **Serves 4**

1 cup fresh, or vacuum-packed, firm tofu (see page 48)
1½ cups rice flour

For the sauce:
2 tbsp. potato starch
4 tbsp. Japanese soy sauce
4 tbsp. mirin (sweet rice wine)
6 tbsp. sugar

Preparation time: 50 minutes

310 cal. per person

1 Dip the tofu briefly in cold water, pat it dry, then purée in a blender. Transfer to a bowl and fold in the rice flour.

2 With moistened hands, shape the tofu into 24 balls, uncovered, for about 5 minutes. Thread the balls onto eight wooden skewers, placing three on each skewer.

3 To make the sauce, dissolve the potato starch in water. Bring the soy sauce, mirin, and sugar to a boil in a saucepan, and continue to cook until the sugar dissolves. Remove the pan from the heat and stir in the potato starch to thicken the sauce. Return briefly to a boil, stirring constantly.

4 Transfer the sauce to a shallow bowl. Holding the skewers, coat the tofu balls with the sauce. Serve them on four individual plates, arranging two tofu skewers on each plate.

Note: Serve as a dessert or afternoon snack accompanied by green tea.

Sweet Potato Balls

Easy • Snack   **Satsuma-imo no chakin-shibori**   **Serves 4**

450 g sweet potatoes
1 to 2 tbsp. matcha (powdered green tea)
2 tbsp. sugar

Preparation time: 45 minutes

130 cal. per serving

1 Peel the sweet potatoes and cut them into pieces. Soak the pieces in water for about 10 minutes, then drain them. Fill a saucepan with water and cook the sweet potatoes, covered, over low heat for about 20 minutes, until tender.

2 Drain the potatoes, reserving 3 tbsp. of the cooking water. Mash the warm potatoes and divide them equally between two bowls.

3 Dissolve the matcha in 1½ tbsp. of the reserved potato water and stir into one bowl of mashed potato. Dissolve the sugar in the remaining potato water and stir it into the other bowl of potato. Leave both portions to cool completely.

4 Place a heaped tablespoon of the matcha-flavored mixture in the middle of a 8-in. square piece of aluminum foil.

5 Gather together the four edges of the foil and twist them to wrap the mixture in the piece of foil.

6 Using both hands, shape the mixture into a small ball, then carefully unwrap it and place on a plate. Repeat the process until all the matcha mixture is used up.

7 Prepare the sugar mixture in the same way. Arrange the balls on four serving plates, giving each portion two balls of each flavor.

Note: Sweet potato balls are a popular tea-time snack in Japan.

Suggested Menus

The Japanese menu does not follow such a strict order as in Europe. Often, all the dishes are served to the same time. Since variety counts for a great deal, it is important to serve as many different dishes as possible. A loaded plate is unacceptable to the Japanese. They find it boring and also contrary to their esthetic sensitivities. That is why visually pleasing presentation is so crucial.

Each type of food is served separately. Fish, vegetables, and rice never appear on the same plate. By presenting each food on its own small dish, platter, or bowl, each food is valued for itself. Unlike Westerners, the Japanese do not use matching dinner services. They are quite happy with a miscellany of different plates, bowls, and serving dishes. Many Japanese families use different crockery for the various times of year. In summer, for example, they use pale, delicate glass or porcelain, and keep dark, heavy china or stoneware for the colder seasons.

If you try the following menus, you will soon gain a feeling for which dishes go together. Pickles are often served with food. These can be bought ready-made from specialty food stores. Since this book does not include recipes for pickles, they are marked with an asterisk. The same applies to fresh fruits, which are the most usual dessert.

The quantities given in the recipes assume that several dishes will be served at the same time. If you want to prepare other menu combinations, including some European dishes, for example, these quantities are enough for an appetizer. Make double the quantity for an entrée.

Quick menus for 4

Chicken Teriyaki	90
Tofu and Wakame Soup	30
Rice	—
Fresh fruits *	

Sesame Spinach	65
Pickles *	—
Egg Soup	34
Fried Flounder	105
Rice	—
Fresh fruits*	—

Fried Tofu	48
Marinated Tuna	117
Miso Soup	37
Fresh fruits*	—

Menus to prepare in advance

Layered Egg Cake	56
Eggplant with Chicken (cold)	70
Boiled Duck (variation)	88
Rice	—
Adzuki Bean Jelly	134

Boiled Daikon	69
Eggplant with Chicken (cold)	70
Broiled Salmon	102
Miso Soup with Beef (variation)	37
Tofu Balls	137

Layered Egg Cake	56
Marinated Duck	94
Salmon and Tofu Soup	40
Rice	—
Adzuki Bean Jelly	134

Pickled Sardines	116
Salsify with Sesame Seeds	68
Boiled Belly of Pork	87
Rice	—
Fresh fruits*	—

Layered Egg Cake	56
Deep-fried Tofu (variation)	48
Vegetable Stew	64
Rice	—
Fresh fruits*	—

Lunch menus

Eggplant with Chicken (cold)	70
Noodles with Tempura	44
Fresh fruits (for example, melon)	—

Sesame Spinach	65
Rice	—
Tofu Soup with Chicken	41
Fresh fruits*	—

Pickled Sardines	116
Udon Noodle Soup	43
Sweet Rice Croquettes	128
Miso Soup	37

Dinner menus

Marinated Tuna	116
Deep-fried Chicken Legs	97
Fish with Noodle Stuffing	118
Miso Soup with Vegetables	37
Pickles *	—
Adzuki Bean Jelly	134

Pear with Sesame Seeds	60
Yakitori	89
Boiled Daikon	69
Broiled Salmon (serve with Rice)	102
Tofu and Wakame Soup	30
Fresh fruits*	

Layered Egg Cake	56
Deep-fried Tofu (variation)	48
Boiled Beef	97
Rice	—
Miso Soup	37
Fresh fruits*	—
Sesame Spinach	65
Sashimi	100
Fried Tofu	48
Sushi Selection	110, 113
Miso Soup	37
Fresh fruits*	—
Mackerel with Miso	120
Eggplant with Chicken (warm)	70
Chicken in Egg Custard	51
Chicken Teriyaki	90
Rice	—
Clam Soup	32
Ice cream with Bean Sauce	135

Spring menu

Flaky Rolled Omelet	52
Sesame Spinach	65
Broiled Salmon	102
Rice	—
Tofu and Wakame Soup	30
Strawberries or Cherries*	—

Summer menu

Eggplant with Chicken (cold)	70
Chicken in Egg Custard (cold)	51
Cabbage and Steak Salad	66
Rice	—
Ice Cream with Fruit	
(for example, watermelon, figs, or peaches) *	—

Fall menu

Stuffed Shiitake Mushrooms	63
Boiled Daikon	69
Fried Tofu	48
Noodles with Tempura	44
Rice	73
Pickles*	—
Chestnut Cakes	132
kaki (persimmon)*	—

Winter menu

Mackerel with Miso	120
Vegetable Stew	64
Chicken in Egg Custard	51
Duck Teriyaki	88
Rice	—
Miso Soup with Vegetables	37
Mandarin oranges *	—

Menus for special occasions

Boiled duck (variation)	88
Egg Sushi with Shrimp (2 per person)	55
Sashimi	100
Boiled Beef	97
Red Festival Rice	80
Clear Soup with Fish Balls	32
Adzuki Bean Jelly	134
Chicken in Egg Custard	51
Duck Teriyaki	88
Pork Shoulder with Salad	87
Rice and Fish Sushi	113
Clam Soup	32
Ice cream with Bean Sauce	135

Buffet for about 10

Prepare double the quantity shown in the recipes:

Salsify with Sesame Seeds	68
Eggplant with Chicken	70
Sesame Spinach	65
Stuffed Shiitake Mushrooms	63
Sashimi	100
Deep-fried Chicken Legs	97
Chicken Kabobs	89
Broiled Salmon	102
Fried Fillet of Herring	103
Rice	—
Pickles*	—
Fresh fruits*	—
Adzuki Bean Jelly	134

Sake snacks

Eggplant with Chicken	70
Pear with Sesame Seeds	60
Stuffed Shiitake Mushrooms	63
Yakitori	89
Deep-fried Chicken Legs	97
Marinated Tuna	117
Deep-fried Tofu (variation)	48

Glossary

This Glossary is intended as a brief guide to some less familiar cooking terms and ingredients, including words or items found on Japanese menus.

Agar-agar: Known in Japan as kanten, agar-agar is a gelling agent produced from tengusa, a type of red seaweed. It contains no calories and can be used in place of unflavored gelatin.

Aonori: Bright green, flaked seaweed, very good as a seasoning or garnish.

Adzuki beans: Small red beans with a slightly sweet flavor. Also known as aduki or azuki beans. Very popular in Japanese cooking. They are often cooked with sugar to make bean purée, the basis of many desserts and candies. Cooking time for dried adzuki beans can vary, depending on how old they are. To be on the safe side, allow extra time or, alternatively, leave them to soak overnight.

Bamboo shoots: Young shoots of a large bamboo plant, picked before they turn woody. In Asia, bamboo shoots are very widely used in vegetable dishes. In the United States, they are mainly sold in cans, but are sometimes available fresh.

Bonito: Bluefish or bonito is a large member of the tuna family. The fillets are dried and finely chopped. Dashi, basic Japanese broth, is made with bonito and kombu (dried kelp).

Chasoba: Soba noodles flavored with green tea.

Chili peppers: Red or green peppers of the capsicum family, ranging from very hot to mild. Chilies contain volatile oils that can irritate the skin and cause the eyes to burn, so handle with caution and wash your hands immediately after using them. The seeds of the chili are its hottest part; this should be taken into account when using either fresh or dried chili pepper.

Chinese (Napa) cabbage: Cabbage with pale to dark green leaves and no stalks. Originally from China, the cabbage is now cultivated in the U.S., especially in California. It should not be kept for too

long as it soon spoils. In Japan, it is very popular as a stir-fry, hotpot, or salad ingredient.

Daikon: Japanese white radish is long and narrow but not as peppery as the red-skinned variety. it is served, usually cut into very thin strips, with a variety of dishes in Japan, and is said to help digest fatty foods.

Daikon leaves: The leaves from daikon shoots are used to season soups or as a garnish.

Dashi: Basic Japanese broth, made from kombu (dried kelp) and bonito flakes. There are two different types: ichiban dashi (dashi 1) and niban dashi (dashi 2), the latter made from kombu and bonito flakes reserved after cooking Dashi 1.

Enokitake mushrooms: Thin, white mushrooms with long stalks and tiny caps only about ¼-in. in diameter. They are used to flavor hotpots and sukiyaki, these mushrooms are available from specialty food stores and the better supermarkets.

Fugu: The globefish or blowfish whose ovaries, skin, muscles, and especially the liver contain a deadly poison, for which there is no antidote. In Japan, fugu chefs must hold a license, which guarantees their expertise in cutting the fish. Fugu is regarded as special delicacy. However, to avoid any possible risk, it is never served to members of the Japanese Imperial Family.

Ginger: Used in many different ways, ginger is grated as a sauce ingredient, or sliced and pickled for sushi and other dishes. Fresh ginger root will keep in the refrigerator for two weeks.

Gingko nuts: Shiny yellow nut sold fresh in Japan and China but seldom elsewhere. They are available canned from specialty food stores. They are a vital ingredient in Japanese cooking, but the fresh nuts must be cooked before eating.

Glutinous rice: Also known as sticky or sweet rice, and called mochigome in Japanese. It consists of nearly 100 percent starch, and is used to make rice cakes and desserts.

Gobo: Japanese burdock, similar to salsify (oyster plant), but rather tougher.

Gohan: See Rice.

Hanakatsuo: Dried bonito flakes used to make dashi and as a seasoning.

Harusame: Japanese cellophane noodles made from mung beans and eaten with such dishes as sukiyaki. They take about 5 minutes to cook in unsalted water.

Hichimi togarashi: Seven-spice mixture or powder, a powdered blend of hot mustard seed, sesame seed, pepper leaf, poppyseed, canola, hemp seeds, and dried tangerine peel. It is very hot and spicy, and is good sprinkled over grilled and broiled meats.

Hijiki: Long, black seaweed. When cooked, the volume expands fivefold. Hijiki is served on its own or with vegetable dishes. See also page 31.

"Itadakimasu": Meaning literally "I take." The Japanese say this at the beginning of a meal. At the end of the meal, they say "Gochisosama," meaning "The food we have eaten was delicious and nourishing."

Japanese pepper: See Sansho.

Kabocha/Squash: Japanese squash has dark green skin with yellow spots. It is usually no more than 4 inches long and 6 inches in diameter. It is a typical winter vegetable which is used for tempura. It can be baked in the oven or steamed in its skin.

Kanpai: The Japanese equivalent of "Cheers!"

Keta: Also known as salmon caviar, keta is made from the roe of a species of Pacific salmon. The pinkish-red eggs are larger than those of real caviar. It is sold in small pots.

Kobe beef: The best Japanese beef comes from the city of Kobe. The cattle are fattened on grain and beer, and massaged with oil or sake so that the fat penetrates the lean flesh to produce the fine marbling for which the beef is known. The more the marbling, the higher the price.

Kombu: Dried brown seaweed, also known as kelp, used to make dashi. See page 31.

Konnyaku: A jelly-like substance made from the starch of tubers of the devil's tongue plant. It aids digestion and is very low in calories. It is used in soups, vegetable stews, and is also used to make shirataki noodles. It is available canned in Japanese food stores.

Lotus root: The root of the lotus plant with its cream color and interestingly-shaped holes adds a decorative touch to vegetable dishes. It has little taste of its own but is very crunchy. It is sold frozen or canned, and very occasionally fresh, from specialty food stores.

Makisu: Special mats made of bamboo, designed to make it easier to roll sushi.

Matcha: Extremely bitter powdered green tea, used in the tea ceremony.

Mirin: Fermented sweet rice wine, used exclusively for cooking. See also page 90.

Miso: Soybean paste, used as a basis for soups and sauce. See also page 38.

Mitsuba: Three-leaved parsley, whose flavor lies somewhere between that of flat-leaved parsley and celery. It adds a distinctive flavor to soups and various other cooked dishes, as well as salads.

Mochi: Also called kiri mochi, these Japanese rice cakes can be bought ready-made from specialty food stores.

Mugicha: Tea made from toasted barley grains. Served cold, it is enjoyed in Japan as a refreshing summer drink.

Nameko: Paddi-straw mushrooms, tiny wild mushrooms with a slippery coating, which grow on rice straw. They are available canned but can be replaced by shiitake mushrooms.

Nashi: Also known as Japanese or Asian pears or apple-pears. Nashi are round apple-like fruits, available in specialty food stores as well as some greengrocers and supermarkets.

Nori: Seaweed, used mainly for rolling around sushi. Dark green or brown in color, it looks like transparent paper. See also page 31.

Ogura an: Canned cooked Japanese adzuki beans, most often used in order to save time.

Owan: Lidded Japanese soup bowls made from lacquered wood or plastic.

Oyster mushrooms: Fan-shaped mushroom, usually without a stem which grows on trees. The color varies from blue-gray to light brown. Commercially cultivated oyster mushrooms are available all the year round from supermarkets and greengrocers. They add the finishing touch to many dishes.

Pickled Japanese ginger: Thin slices of ginger pickled in vinegar, salt, and sugar. Sold in jars in specialty food stores.

Rice: The mainstay of the Japanese diet. A bowl of rice is always served to accompany the entrée. See also page 75.

Sake: Japanese rice wine, drunk warm or cold. Along with tea, it is the drink must frequently served with food. See also page 122.

Sansho: Thorny Japanese ash often called a pepper tree, though it is not related to the pepper plant. The fresh leaves are used as a soup garnish. Unfortunately, they are very difficult to come by in the West. Sansho pepper, made from the dried, powdered outer husks of the seeds, has the same spicy flavor as the leaves and can be bought in specialty food stores.

Sashimi: Sliced raw fish, served with radish and wasabi. The fish is spread with a little wasabi before being dipped in soy sauce. If you have never tried preparing sahimi, it is best to start with salmon and tuna.

Sesame oil: Oil with a strong aroma and distinctive nutty flavor, best used sparingly. The basic oil of Japanese cuisine, it is used in stir-frying and to add flavor to boiled dishes.

Sesame seeds: Sesame seeds: Both black and white sesame seeds feature in Japanese cooking and are often toasted before use (you can also buy them ready-toasted.) They are often ground using a pestle and mortar to make sesame paste. Ready-made sesame paste (tahini) is available from supermarkets and specialty food stores.

Seven-spice mixture: See Hichimi togarashi.Shiitake mushrooms: Popular oriental mushrooms, which available both fresh and dried in larger supermarkets and greengrocers. Since dried mushrooms have a stronger flavor, they are used in many dishes in preference to the fresh ones.

Shirataki: Thin thread-like noodles made from konnyaku. They take about 2 minutes to cook. Cellophane noodles can be used instead.

Shiso: The aromatic shiso or beefsteak plant has been cultivated in Japan for centuries, as a culinary, medicinal, or ornamental plant, and for producing oil. The leaves have a flavor similar to that of lemon balm or peppermint. They are used whole or chopped as a seasoning. The leaves can sometimes be bought fresh from specialty food stores, but they are very expensive. Lemon balm is a good substitute.

Shungiku: Known as chrysanthemum leaf, since it looks like the leaf of young chrysanthemums. It is available fresh from specialty food stores. It is a sukiyaki ingredient, and is also used for clear soups and miso soups. It tastes rather like leaf spinach.

Soba: These brown noodles made from buckwheat flour are very popular and alleged to have health-giving properties. They should be cooked for about 10 minutes in unsalted water.

Soybeans: These beans are popular throughout Asia. They are used to make a number of products, including soy sauce and tofu, and are also good eaten as a vegetable.

Soy sauce: Japanese soy sauce (shoyu) is produced from soy beans, wheat, sea salt, and water, and is fermented for about six months. Japanese soy sauce is more delicate and less salty than the Chinese brands. It is used as an ingredient in cooking and as a dip.

Su: Mild rice vinegar, mixed with rice to make sushi.

Sukiyaki: Famous beef dish cooked at the table. Beef, tofu, leeks, cellophane noodles and shiitake mushrooms are simmered in a special broth and dipped in raw egg before eating.

Suribachi: Japanese mortar. A stoneware bowl, serrated on the inside, used with a wooden pestle.

Surimi: Pressed fish, such as crab sticks, sold fresh or frozen.

Sushi: Famous Japanese rice titbit. Vinegared rice is spread with a little wasabi (Japanese horseradish) and topped with raw fish. Sushis are always eaten as a Entrée. Before eating, they are dipped in soy sauce. There are countless variations.

Sweet potato: Long tuber with pink or yellow skin. They can be boiled or baked but are also used in sweet dishes.

Tempura: Vegetables and fish coated in batter, deep-fried in oil and served with various dips.

Teriyaki: Seasoning sauce, made from soy sauce, wine and spices, used to marinate meat and fish.

Tofu: Firm soybean curd produced from soy milk. It can be boiled, fried or grilled or made into desserts. Tofu is a very important source of protein in oriental cuisine. See also page 48.

Udon: Thick, white wheat flour noodles. They take about 10 minutes to cook; as they are already salty, there is no need to add salt to the cooking water.

Umeboshi: Pickled or sour Japanese plums, though they actually are a type of apricot pickled before they are ripe. They have a dry, sour flavor, and can be used as a cooking ingredient or eaten raw. Umeboshi are believed to have a purifying effect, so are often served for breakfast in Japan.

Wakame: Brown seaweed, used mainly for soups and salads. See also page 31.

Wasabi: Very hot, green Japanese horseradish, available as either powder or paste, used in sushi and sashimi.

Yakitori: Chicken grilled on skewers. The chicken is dipped in a soy sauce-based marinade before, during and after grilling over charcoal.

Yam: Generic term for a range of tuberous tropical and subtropical plants of the discorea genus. The starchy, glutinous tubers are the tropical equivalent of potatoes. They have a brownish-pink skin and white flesh. They can be roasted, baked or fried like ordinary potatoes.

Yuzu: Japanese citrus fruit with a bitter, rather dry flesh and a fragrant rind, tasting rather like lime. Yuzu is used in Japan as a flavoring, sometimes in savory sauces, or as a garnish.

CONVERSION CHART

These figures are not exact equivalents, but have been rounded up or down slightly to make measuring easier.

Weight Equivalents		Volume Equivalents	
Metric	Imperial	Metric	Imperial
15 g	½ oz.	8 cl	3 fl. oz.
30 g	1 oz.	12,5 cl	4 fl. oz.
60 g	2 oz.	15 cl	½ cup
90 g	3 oz.	17,5 cl	6 fl. oz.
125 g	¼ lb.	25 cl	8 fl. oz.
150 g	5 oz.	30 cl	1 cup
200 g	7 oz.	35 cl	12 fl. oz.
250 g	½ lb.	45 cl	1½ cup
350 g	¾ lb.	50 cl	16 fl. oz.
500 g	1 lb.	60 cl	2 cups
1 kg	2 to 2¼ lb.	1 liter	35 fl. oz.

Recipe Index

Cover: A bowl of mussels in miso soup, delicately garnished with thin strips of leek (recipe, page 38), provides the perfect culinary and decorative accompaniment to chicken teriyaki – a popular grilled dish using rice wines and soy sauce as flavoring (recipe, page 90) – and little tuna fish and cucumber sushi (recipe, page 110). A glass of warmed sake completes the picture.

Published in the United States by
Thunder Bay Press
An imprint of the Advantage Publishers Group
5880 Oberlin Drive
San Diego, CA 92121-4794
www.advantagebooksonline.com

Published originally under the title
Küchen der Welt: Japan
© Copyright 1994 Gräfe und Unzer Verlag GmbH, Munich
English translation by Isabel Varea for Ros Schwartz Translations, London
American adaptation: Josephine Bacon for American Pie, London

Library of Congress Cataloging-in-Publication Data.
Hayamizu, Kiyoshi.
Cuisines of the world: Japan/Kiyoshi Hayamizu, Yuhei Hoshino. p.cm.
Translation of: Küchen der Welt. Japan.
ISBN 1-57145-260-5
1. Cookery, Japanese. I. Hoshino, Yuhei.
II. Title.
TX724.5.J3 H385 2000. 641.5952–dc21

1 2 3 4 5   00 01 02 03 04

Color reproduction by Fotolito Longo, Bolzano, Italy
Typeset by Satz + Litho Sporer KG, Augsburg, Germany
Printed and bound by Artes Gráficas Toledo S.A.U.
D.L.TO: 246-2000

GRÄFE UND UNZER

EDITORS: Dr. Stephanie von Werz-Kovacs and Birgit Rademacker
Sub-Editor: Angela Hermann
Designer: Konstantin Kern
Recipes tested by: Marianne Obermayr, Renate Neis, Marianne Stadler, Traute Hatterscheid
Production: VerlagsService Neuberger & Schaumann GmbH, Heimstetten
Cartography: Huber, Munich

NORTH AMERICAN EDITION:
Managing Editor: JoAnn Padgett
Project Editor: Elizabeth McNulty

Kiyoshi Hayamizu trained as a chef in Tokyo and worked in several of the city's restaurants before moving to Europe. He is now chef at the Daitokai restaurant in Düsseldorf. His coauthor **Yuhei Hoshino** has a similar background, having gained valuable experience at a number of Tokyo restaurants before also moving to Europe, where he is now chef in charge of all the Kikkoman and Daitokai restaurants.

Foodphotography Eising Pete A. Eising and Susanne Eising specialize in food photography and work closely with a food photography agency in Germany and Switzerland. Their clients include publishers, ad agencies, and industrial companies. Food and props stylist for this volume was Martina Görlach, assisted by Ulla Krause.

Heike Czygan, who did the illustrations for this book, is a designer working for a leading publishing house in Munich. She is fascinated by ancient Oriental art styles, having lived in both China and Japan.

Picture Credits

Color illustrations: Heike Czygan

All photographs by Food photography Eising unless indicated below:

Cover: Graham Kirk, London. 4 (4) (Tokyo teenagers: Toshugu shrine festival, Nikko), 4-5, top (Akihabara district, Tokyo): Paul Spierenburg, Kiel. 4-5, center (No theater, Nara): Rainer Hackenberg, Cologne. 5, 8-9 (the Great Buddha of Kamakura): Erhard Pansegrau, Berlin. 10 (2), 11: Rainer Hackenberg, Cologne. 12, top: Erhard Pansegrau, Berlin; bottom: Paul Spierenburg, Kiel. 13 top: Silvestris Fotoservice, Kastl; 13 bottom, 14: Paul Spierenburg, Kiel. 15, 16 bottom,: Erhard Pansegrau, Berlin. 16 top, 17 (2): Rainer Hackenberg, Cologne. 18-19: Broth Food Eising, Munich. 19, top: Paul Spierenburg, Kiel; bottom: Japanese Tourist Office, Frankfurt. 20, top: Paul Spierenburg, Kiel; bottom: Erhard Pansegrau, Berlin. 21, 22 (2): Rainer Hackenberg, Cologne. 22-3: Erhard Pansegrau, Cologne. 23: Broth Food Eising, Munich. 24: Paul Spierenburg, Kiel. 25, top: Silvestris Fotoservice, Kastl; bottom, 31: Rainer Hackenberg, Cologne. 75: Erhard Pansegrau, Berlin. 122: Paul Spierenburg, Kiel.

The authors would also like to thank the following for supplying props:

Firma Kyoto Porzellan GmbH, Immermannstr. 26, 40210 Düsseldorf.
A Warnecke, Rungedamm 37, 21035 Hamburg.
Japanalia, Herzogstr. 7, 80803 Munich.
Kikkoman Trading Europe GmbH, Düsseldorf.
Kikkoman & Daitokai (Europe), Düsseldorf.